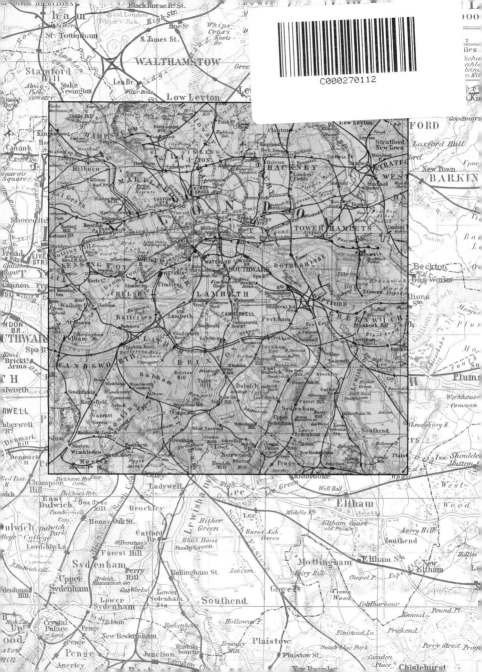

LONDON
COCKTAILS

AN ELEGANT COLLECTION OF OVER 100 RECIPES FROM A TO ZED

FELIPE SCHRIEBERG

CIDER MILL PRESS

BOOK PUBLISHERS
KENNEBUNKPORT, MAINE

13-Digit ISBN: 978-1-60433-956-7
10-Digit ISBN: 1-60433-956-X

This book may be ordered by mail from the publisher. Please include $5.99 for postage and handling. Please support your local bookseller first!

Books published by Cider Mill Press Book Publishers are available at special discounts for bulk purchases in the United States by corporations, institutions, and other organizations. For more information, please contact the publisher.

Cider Mill Press Book Publishers
"Where good books are ready for press"
PO Box 454
12 Spring Street
Kennebunkport, Maine 04046
Visit us online!
cidermillpress.com

Typography: AW Conqueror Carved, Avenir, Copperplate, Sackers, Warnock

Photography Credits on pages 349–350

Printed in China

2 3 4 5 6 7 8 9 0

CONTENTS

INTRODUCTION

London is a place where tradition combines and clashes with re-invention. Where towering glass skyscrapers are raised a stone's throw from stately Victorian buildings. This constant state of redevelopment means that many of the city's neighborhoods are unrecognizable from 20 or even 10 years ago as continuous investment has led to new buildings, new commercial and residential areas, and new businesses. The ancient sits next to the modern, packed like commuters on London's famous/infamous Tube, a juxtaposition as adored and detested by the city's residents as that mode of transport. People from all corners of the world, from all walks of life, have turned London into a vibrant, multicultural, cosmopolitan hub.

London's cocktail bars follow the pattern of the city. The cocktail scene these days is buzzing, and though new bars and projects are constantly emerging, customers also continue to pack the floors of ancient institutions that have served drinks for more than a century.

Current cocktail trends in the city reflect that balance between old and new. There is a renewed focus on the provenance of ingredients, and a return to working with classic recipes. More recently, custom-batched ingredients and cocktails that have been prepared in advance have become popular, involving preparations that are made with customer service in mind, as they would be impossible to make quickly on demand. Innovations in methods and flavor combinations are commonplace. London is in the midst of a golden age of cocktails.

A BRIEF HISTORY OF COCKTAILS (AND GIN) IN LONDON

The history of London's cocktails begins with gin. At the Tate Britain museum in Vauxhall lies a reproduction of one the world's most famous prints—a humble public service announcement.

William Hogarth's "Gin Lane," first published in 1751 (and shown to the right), depicts a cartoonish state of absolute societal degeneration in the slum of St. Giles, a neighborhood north of Covent Garden that is now a section of the glitzy West End. Its miserable, poverty-stricken residents are a mess. A boy fights with a dog over a bone while a drunk mother lets her baby fall to its doom. A hanged corpse is visible in the window of a crumbling tenement. The title makes clear the reason for this gruesome state of affairs: gin.

"Gin Lane" (and its companion print, "Beer Street," extolling the societal benefits of beer) appeared at the tail end of a dark, 31-year period known as the Gin Craze (1720-1751), when the city as a whole stumbled along in a drunken fog.

In her 2012 book, *Gin: A Global History*, drinks journalist Lesley Jacobs Solmonson reports that in London "at any given time one out of every four residents—essentially all of the city's poor—was completely and utterly incoherent." This situation was initially fuelled by a ban on trading with the French. The inability to procure French brandy, combined with a 1690 parliamentary act "encouraging the distilling of brandy and spirits from corn" let loose a flood of cheap booze into the market, and the additions of imported Dutch genever and local production of moonshine eventually drowned London in liquor.

Several centuries later, Londoners are enjoying a new period sometimes referred to as the Gin Renaissance. The number of distilleries in England has increased from 23 in 2010 to 166 as of January 2019. However, rather than the cheap moonshine of yore, these days

London's consumers and bartenders are obsessed not only with the subtle and delicate aromas that new gin products radiate, but also with the cocktails they grace—and never have they tasted so good.

So how did we get from "craze" to "renaissance?" To a degree, it starts with horses.

Where the word "cocktail" first emerged is a bit of a mystery, but it is likely linked to the practice of trimming horses' tails to signify they were not thoroughbreds. When they were offered for sale, owners would apply a ginger suppository to ensure they behaved in an energetic, frisky manner, showing off their "cocked tail." One plausible theory to explain the word's transfer to drinks is that by diluting a spirit with other ingredients, it was no longer a "purebred," therefore it was a "cocktail."

Furthermore, these theories are upheld in a 1798 printed reference to a cocktail-as-drink when the *Morning Post and Gazetteer* ran a story about a pub owner who erased his customers' tabs after winning a lottery. A few days later, the paper satirically reported the details of 17 politicians' drinks tabs, Prime Minister William Pitt's among them: "Mr. Pitt, two petit vers of 'L'huile de Venus,' Ditto, one of 'perfeit amour,' Ditto, 'cock-tail' (vulgarly called ginger)." In this case, the "cock-tail" refers to a mix of gin and ginger syrup, though taking into account Britons' enduring love for wordplay, it's not hard to imagine that something else may have been implied.

In any case, the first written definition of a cocktail was recorded in *The Balance and Columbian Repository* newspaper of Hudson, New York, in 1806: "a stimulating liquor composed of any kind of sugar, water and bitters, vulgarly called a bittered sling."

BIRTH OF THE MODERN COCKTAIL

Eventually, "bittered slings" transcended their base origins and became something fancier, even enjoyed by royalty (see the Soyer au Champagne, page 30). Gin palaces were founded in the early 19th century, with drinks being served in gaudy, garish, and colorful establishments, shelters that allowed Londoners to escape the miserable and dirty city of the period. (Charles Dickens is arguably the greatest chronicler of London during this time.) In these gin palaces, according to Dickens, "compounds" were served—slings with added syrup and bitters.

In the 1840s, along came a French chef who took things further. Alexis Benoit Soyer gained renown in London for his over-the-top feasts, as well as his over-the-top drinks, some of which would earn pride of place in a bar today. Londoners of all stripes couldn't get enough of Soyer's concoctions. He created the world's first blue drinks and jello shots. His other innovations included the world's first soup kitchens, conceived when he traveled to Ireland to feed the victims of its Great Famine, and the creation of innovative field stoves to help feed dying soldiers in the Crimean War. (The British army kept the design for 120 years.) The godfather of American cocktails, Jerry "The Professor" Thomas, incorporated some of Soyer's recipes into his repertoire.

From 1863, the phylloxera aphid plague, imported from the Americas, temporarily wiped out Cognac, wine, and Sherry production in Europe, opening the way for cocktails to receive more attention. Sweeter American drinks such as the Mint Julep were popular in London, but there also was a drive toward British tipples. Books such as *Cups and Their Customs* by Henry Porter and George Roberts (1863) and *The Gentleman's Table Guide* by E. Ricket and C. Thomas (1871) offered an extensive selection of drinks.

From the late 19th century, the hotels in the center of town led the cocktail charge, especially those around Piccadilly Circus. The Savoy is a classic example of an institution of this time—and it's still serving drinks today. It was in the Criterion's Long Bar that Dr. John H. Watson would meet Sherlock Holmes in Sir Arthur Conan Doyle's 1887 tome *A Study in Scarlet.* (While the characters were fictional, the bar was real enough.) These establishments set the template that many hotel bars in London continue to follow, albeit updated for the contemporary world.

Then came Prohibition, outlawing alcohol in the United States and allowing London to truly take the lead over New York in cocktail innovation. Prohibition also drove English barman Harry Craddock back home after a few years of plying his trade in New York. He went on to become the head bartender of The Savoy and, in 1930, wrote *The Savoy Cocktail Book.* Containing multiple recipes that are considered classics today, legendary bartender and drinks writer Gary Regan called Craddock's work "probably the most important cocktail book of the 20th century."

After World War II, however, the demand for quality cocktails dissipated, victim to the rock-and-roll sensibilities of the Swinging '60s and the the economic recession of the '70s.

After those troubled times, along came Dick Bradsell. Starting in the 1980s, he studied and brought back classic cocktails and, perhaps more importantly, trained the barflies who would establish the hippest London bars in the '90s, driving not only an explosion of interest in quality drinks and ingredients, but also helping to rejuvenate a drinks, bar, and hospitality community that has been growing ever since. Bradsell was a master technician as well, creating cocktails such as the Bramble, Espresso Martini, and the Russian Spring Punch that are now famous worldwide.

LONDON TODAY

These days, many of London's drinks masters have been trained by either Bradsell or one of his apprentices who cut their teeth in the '90s. Other well-known names have made their way to London either to hone their skills or practice their trade in the world's best drinks city, breaking new boundaries in the process.

One of today's top bar entrepreneurs, the award-winning Ryan Chetiyawardana (also known as Mr. Lyan), shocked the London drinks scene when he eschewed perishables, fruit, and ice in his drinks, which were often prepared in advance to deal quickly with orders. He emphasized service, and promoted a sustainability-focused alternative to the usual way of doing business.

Another example is Ago Perrone, a native of the region surrounding Italy's Lake Como. Perrone relaunched the stunning and globally acclaimed Connaught Bar in 2008, just five years after stepping off a plane at Heathrow armed with little more than a smattering of English, a scruffy beard, and his immense talent. His focus: top-quality service, creative approaches to classic drinks, and the addition of subtle but classy theatrics that are seamlessly integrated into the customer experience.

Czech Alex Kratena and Norwegian Monica Berg, both celebrated names in the drinks industry, are driving London wild with their new Old Street bar Tayēr + Elementary.

London hosts an enormous variety of bars, each with a unique approach and philosophy. Some attack cocktails the way the world's best restaurants attack cooking: with a molecular approach, using technologically advanced equipment. Others have gone the opposite way, aiming to create the best drinks through minimalism, confining themselves to a maximum of three ingredients. Still others seek to place their own subtle twists on classics, or perhaps they'll push a specific theme to

its absolute limit, or maybe focus on using only the finest ingredients.

Social media has also influenced operations in a number of bars, as becoming viral on Instagram sometimes means focusing on a visual or theatrical angle for drinks. The overwhelming popularity of gin also has meant that vodka, all the rage in the '90s, has taken a back seat. Other spirits, such as rum or whisky, are receiving more attention than in the past.

However, all of the city's top bars—those that the London drinks industry respects most—obsessively emphasize the importance of customer service over everything else. Customers are as likely to remember a unique, positive experience as they are a top-quality drink. Bad customer service also means that a top-quality cocktail is that much harder to enjoy or appreciate, rendering moot the point of going to a bar in the first place. It is this concept that unites London's best bars, more than any overarching philosophy, trend, or fad.

It also means that London will continue as a global cocktail capital–arguably *the* global cocktail capital—for many years to come. Join me in raising a glass to that.

DRINK LIKE A LONDONER

Be picky about gin

We're in the Gin Renaissance, and Londoners are taking gin more seriously than ever. Don't be afraid to ask for gin recommendations from the bartender, even when ordering a G & T.

Everyone loves an interactive alcohol experience

Interactive alcohol experiences are a "thing" at the moment. Try the prison-themed "Alco-traz" that's all the rage right now, or a drink-soaked, immersive murder mystery night. Or perhaps a gin-making workshop, where you pick the botanicals that define the spirit you eventually bottle for yourself, is more up your alley.

Keep current on the new bars

New establishments open up all the time in London. Many websites and blogs track what's happening and what's hip.

People are drinking outdoors, even in lousy weather

The weather isn't very good in Britain so you may as well accept it and join the party outside.

Bottomless brunches tend to offer bubbly drinks

Loads of places in London do a bottomless brunch on Sunday, which almost always includes unlimited Prosecco.

Pints are sacred

It is acceptable to enjoy a pint of beer in almost any social situation, no matter the occasion.

Rounds

Always offer to buy them and don't duck out when it's your turn.

Know your locals

It's important to figure out your favorite pub for a pint and bar for a cocktail near where you lay your head in case you need a night out on short notice.

Get a greasy meal at the end of the night

There is little more delicious than a cheeky kebab or cheesy chips at the end of the night, and they help soak up the booze, too.

It is acceptable to turn up to work hungover (most of the time)

Your boss will probably be feeling rough, too, especially if you were out together.

HOW TO SET UP A HOME BAR

So, you want to make high-quality cocktails? Here's how to prep a good, basic home bar, enabling you to make many of the drinks featured in this book, as well as any standard cocktail. Remember to start simple. Then, once you've gotten the hang of things, you can start experimenting with expanding your stock and equipment. Not including stock, you should be able to get everything you need for under $300. And remember to always use ingredients whose taste you actually enjoy.

Tools

Mixing Glass: This is essentially a large glass where you'll put the ingredients to stir them. Ideally, it will have a little lip, making it easy to pour from.

Mixing/Bar Spoon: A long, thin spoon, typically with a spiralled shaft, designed for stirring drinks. Some cocktail recipes will call for a bar spoon of certain ingredients, which is equal to 1 teaspoon.

Shaker: Possibly the most important tool in mixology. You'll shake your ingredients together in it to mix and chill as required. There are different types on the market but it is probably better to avoid one with a built-in strainer; those are harder to clean and tricky for handling egg whites and other ingredients.

Strainer: To separate certain solid bits from your liquid as you pour. A Hawthorne strainer is a great choice, as it can be securely fitted over the shaker. A julep strainer, which has a perforated surface, is another widely available option.

Fine Strainer: A mesh strainer that catches smaller particles, like fruit pieces and ice flecks.

Cheesecloth: This is to filter your drinks and, occasionally, syrups as thoroughly as possible. A few recipes call for this, although coffee filters can also provide the desired results.

Jiggers: Handy little measuring utensils that ensure you get your ingredient proportions right. Make sure you get ones with the measurements you think you will need most.

Juice Press: Mostly for making fresh lemon and lime juice, which you will need to do often.

Muddler: A bartender's pestle, used to mash fruit, herbs, and spices in the bottom of a glass or shaker to help release their flavor.

Ice Trays: Various recipes call for different types of ice. Ideally, have trays that can do normal-sized cubes, spheres, and larger blocks. An ice crusher, for crushed ice, can be useful, too.

Glassware: At the very least, have some rocks glasses, but highball glasses are also useful, as are coupes and/or cocktail glasses. These will cover almost all types of cocktails and the glasses that they would require (or can replace other types of glasses with a similar profile).

SPECIALIZED EQUIPMENT

Vacuum Bags: A bag that allows no air through. Useful for infusions, both with and without sous vide.

Sous Vide Cooker: A device that allows you to heat water to a specific temperature, with extreme precision. It's excellent for infusing liquids intended for use in cocktail making.

Spirits

Gin: London Dry gin is your "standard" style, usually with juniper and citrus notes leading the way. Old Tom Gin is also useful, and will tend to be sweeter as well as richer in different flavors.

Vodka: Best is a liquor of higher quality that has a clean flavor and is (relatively) easy to drink.

Rum: A white rum provides a softer profile and sweetness, best for Daiquiris and Mojitos. A dark or spiced rum is necessary for any tiki drink, and will also provide much fuller flavors than white rum.

Tequila and Mezcal: The former is necessary for Margaritas, and other beloved cocktails. Mezcal is smokier, and can be experimented with in cocktails where peated Scotch is called for.

Whisk(e)y: A bourbon is always useful because it is usually very sweet. Rye will tend to be richer and spicier, and has more caramel notes than bourbon. Scotch is versatile; you will get all kinds of flavors. A good blended Scotch will have a little sweetness, a bit of fruit, and full-bodied richness. Peated Scotches will add a unique, unparalleled smoke. Irish whiskey tends to be creamier with more vanilla notes. The spelling of this word in this book varies based on the origin of the spirit in question.

Brandy and Cognac: Many older recipes call for one of them. On the whole, they are more intense and woody, and could replace Scotch in some cases. Ideally, use VSOP or better.

Liqueurs

Orange Liqueurs: Whether triple sec, Cointreau, or Grand Marnier, these always will be useful.

Dry and Sweet Vermouth: At a minimum, you want one bottle of each on hand at all times. Martini & Rossi is one of the go-to sweet vermouths and Noilly Prat is a common dry one.

Cherry Liqueur: Luxardo maraschino cherry liqueur is common, but Cherry Heering is great, too.

St-Germain: A popular elderflower liqueur that adds unique floral notes to a drink.

Sparkling Wine: Sparkling cocktails are becoming more popular in London so it might be useful to have a spare bottle of Champagne or sparkling wine handy.

Bitters: You will often use Angostura but there is a wide world of choices that provide many flavors.

Other Elements

Citrus: At the minimum, have a good amount of lemons and limes on hand so you can make fresh juice and garnishes. Don't hesitate to go for grapefruits and oranges, too, if you think you might use them.

Simple Syrup: Place 1 part sugar and 1 part water in a saucepan and bring to a simmer, stirring gently until the sugar dissolves. Let the mix cool before bottling and storing in the refrigerator for up to a month.

Rich Simple Syrup: The same process as above, only it uses 2 parts sugar to 1 part water. It will last up to 6 months in the refrigerator.

Juices: Apple, pineapple, cranberry, tomato—anything you like the taste of, really.

Carbonated Mixers: Quality tonic water, because Gin & Tonics always are called for. But if you have the space, soda water, ginger ale, and cola are good to have on hand.

Herbs: Basil and mint are great for garnishes and easy infusions. Rosemary and thyme can also add some great flavors. Feel free to experiment with any others you might like.

Techniques and Terms in Recipes

Shake: If the recipe calls for the cocktail to be shaken (and many in this book do), make sure you fill your shaker with ice cubes (unless instructed otherwise) after adding your ingredients. Shake vigorously for 10 to 20 seconds.

Dry Shake: A dry shake means that you shake the ingredients without adding any ice to the cocktail shaker. This will help viscous ingredients—like egg whites—emulsify.

Strain: Ensures that the ice (or other chunky things) from a shaker or mixing glass do not get into your glass.

Double-Strain: Pouring the contents of the cocktail shaker through a fine strainer or a mesh strainer in addition to the strainer that will remove the chunky elements.

Stir: Another common mixing method. Fill a mixing glass with ice and pour in the required ingredients. Using a bar spoon, find its balance point (usually around two-thirds up the spoon), and use a pushing-and-pulling motion while rotating the wrist to ensure that the ingredients are mixed together without agitation. It takes a little practice to do well, but once you get it, it's a useful skill.

Mist: Simply put the liquid that needs to be misted into a spray bottle or fit an atomizer top onto the bottle containing the liquid in order to gently spray the mist around the glass or on top of the drink.

CLASSIC

COCKTAILS

SOYER AU CHAMPAGNE • BLACK VELVET

• THE JOHN COLLINS • BUCK'S FIZZ •

HANKY PANKY • WHITE LADY •

CORPSE REVIVER #2 • VESPER MARTINI

• ESPRESSO MARTINI • BRAMBLE •

THE BREAKFAST MARTINI

ondon has long been a global capital, so it is no surprise that some of the world's best-known drinks were first enjoyed in the city's cosmopolitan bars. The 11 cocktails showcased here represent a panoramic history of extraordinary flavor innovation in London and are a testament to the work and vision of the pioneers who created them.

Some of these cocktails, such as Dick Bradsell's Espresso Martini, represent the rewards of constant experimentation. Others, such as Ada Coleman's Hanky Panky, were born in a flash of inspiration. Most importantly, these recipes are artifacts of their time, reflecting wider socioeconomic trends impacting London and Great Britain when they were first served. In part, that explains why most of these recipes, spanning more than 150 years, are known to bartenders worldwide. As you enjoy one or the other, appreciate not only its exceptional flavors, but the little piece of history in your glass.

– SOYER AU CHAMPAGNE –

Alexis Soyer was quite a character. Perhaps best described as a culinary revolutionary, he was a French chef who made his name across the Channel, in London. His accomplishments include inventing soup kitchens during the Irish famine, field stoves during the Crimean War, and possibly some of the first-ever cocktails in the sense that we understand them today.

In 1851, he also opened his incredible restaurant, Soyer's Universal Symposium of All Nations. Standing where the legendary Royal Albert Hall is now, the restaurant showcased his food-and-drink talents. Although, sadly, the restaurant didn't last long and was a financial flop, this drink featuring vanilla ice cream and Champagne went on to live a long life after it graced Soyer's menu. Apparently, Queen Victoria loved it.

This particular recipe dates back to an *Esquire* article originally published in 1937.

GLASSWARE: Large tumbler
GARNISH: Pineapple slice, orange slice,
lemon slice, 2 cherries, and 2 strawberries

- 2 tablespoons vanilla ice cream
- 2 dashes brandy
- 2 dashes Curaçao
- 2 dashes Luxardo maraschino cherry liqueur
- 2 oz. Champagne, to top

1. Scoop the ice cream into glass. Add the brandy, Curaçao, and Luxardo.
2. Top with Champagne, garnish with the fruits, and serve with a spoon and straw.

– BLACK VELVET –

When Prince Albert died of typhoid fever in 1861, a mourning Queen Victoria famously wore nothing but black for the rest of her life. Out of respect, the Brooks Club in London created this simple drink that same year, its dark color similarly honoring the life of the Prince Consort, with the stout shrouding the Champagne. It's recommended to use a dry Champagne, such as Brut, to cut effectively through the stout.

GLASSWARE: Champagne flute

GARNISH: None

- **1 part stout (usually Guinness)**
- **1 part Champagne**

1. Chill the champagne flute.

2. Slowly pour both ingredients into the chilled glass simultaneously.

– THE JOHN COLLINS –

The name for this cocktail came from a poem written by Frank and Charles Sheridan about a head waiter at a London bar called Limmer's. The earliest written recipe for the drink is dated 1869, though it's likely the drink itself is older.

Though the John Collins is known as a gin drink, legendary bartender Gary "Gaz" Regan points to another interpretation from 1906, where drinks authority Louis Muckensturm argued that Dutch genever was actually the main spirit. Feel free to try both and choose your preference. This version, however, is officially sanctioned by the International Bartenders Association.

GLASSWARE: Collins glass
GARNISH: Lemon slice, maraschino cherry,
and dash of Angostura Bitters

- 3 parts gin or genever
- 2 parts fresh lemon juice
- 1 part Simple Syrup (see page 24)
- 4 parts soda water

1. Add all of the ingredients to a highball glass filled with ice and stir gently until chilled.

2. Garnish with the lemon slice, maraschino cherry, and dash of Angostura Bitters.

– BUCK'S FIZZ –

oes this qualify as a cocktail? Perhaps not, yet it has a long history with nebulous origins. Supposedly, it was created in 1921 by Pat McGarry, the first bartender at the London gentlemen's fixture the Buck's Club. Legend has it that it was invented to give club members an excuse to drink earlier in the day. Even now, it's still served at the club. Variations include adding gin and cherry liqueur.

The key to a successful Buck's Fizz: ingredients of exceptional quality. Various Champagnes will affect the taste differently, as will high-quality or freshly squeezed juice rather than the cheap stuff from a carton. And remember, the difference between a Buck's Fizz and a Mimosa (created four years later in Paris) is that the latter is equal parts orange juice and Champagne.

GLASSWARE: Champagne flute
GARNISH: Orange twist

- **1 part fresh orange juice**
- **2 parts Champagne**

1. Pour the orange juice into the champagne flute, top with the Champagne, and garnish with an orange twist.

– HANKY PANKY –

The Hanky Panky is the brainchild of Ada "Coley" Coleman, the renowned head bartender at The Savoy's American Bar and one of only two women to hold that position. Among her regular customers was the legendary actor and cocktail connoisseur Sir Charles Hawtrey, for whom she was trying to create the perfect cocktail as a pick-him-up after a hard day. After he tried this invention, he exclaimed: "By Jove, that is the real hanky-panky!" The name stuck.

This particular recipe comes from *The Savoy Cocktail Book* written by Coleman's successor, the equally renowned Harry Craddock, who likely knew Ada well, as their time at The Savoy overlapped before she retired.

GLASSWARE: Cocktail glass
GARNISH: Orange twist

- 1½ oz. dry gin
- 1½ oz. sweet vermouth
- 2 dashes Fernet-Branca

1. Add the ingredients to a cocktail shaker filled with ice, shake vigorously until chilled, and strain into the cocktail glass.

2. Garnish with the orange twist.

- WHITE LADY -

The best-known version of the White Lady probably belongs to Craddock, former head bartender of The Savoy. Hence, I've chosen his recipe here. That said, the original recipe for the White Lady likely belongs to Dundonian bartender Harry MacElhone, who created the drink in 1919 while working in London at Ciro's Club before further refining it after he went to Paris.

A competing origin story from The Savoy insists that not only was the drink invented there, but was named after F. Scott Fitzgerald's platinum-blonde wife, Zelda.

Most modern versions of the White Lady include an egg white, so that's optional here, as is the garnish.

GLASSWARE: Champagne coupe
GARNISH: Lemon twist (optional)

- **1 egg white (optional)**
- **2 oz. gin**
- **1 oz. Cointreau**
- **1 oz. fresh lemon juice**

1. Chill the champagne coupe.

2. If using the egg white, combine all of the ingredients in a cocktail shaker containing no ice and dry shake for 20 seconds. Add ice and shake vigorously until chilled.

3. Strain into the chilled glass and, if using, garnish with the lemon twist.

- CORPSE REVIVER #2 -

Although the mention of a Corpse Reviver cocktail recipe dates back to 1871, Craddock's *The Savoy Cocktail Book* laid out a number of variations on this theme when it was published in 1930. This is considered to be the best, and you can still enjoy it today at The Savoy. Craddock notes that "four of these taken in quick succession will unrevive the corpse again." In the original recipe, he calls for "Kina Lillet" but that product no longer exists, so Lillet Blanc is the commonly accepted substitute.

GLASSWARE: Cocktail glass
GARNISH: Citrus twist

- 1 oz. dry gin
- 1 oz. Cointreau
- 1 oz. Lillet Blanc
- 1 oz. fresh lemon juice
- 1 dash absinthe

1. Add the all of the ingredients to a cocktail shaker filled with ice, shake vigorously until chilled, and strain into the cocktail glass.

2. Garnish with the citrus twist.

" **A** dry martini," he said. "One. In a deep champagne goblet."
"Oui, monsieur."

"Just a moment. Three measures of Gordon's, one of vodka, half a measure of Kina Lillet. Shake it very well until it's ice-cold, then add a large thin slice of lemon peel. Got it?"

"Certainly, monsieur." The barman seemed pleased with the idea.

This is how the unusual Vesper Martini was born, in the pages of Ian Fleming's 1953 book *Casino Royale*, with James Bond delivering strict instructions for his order. Later, he stipulates that grain vodka (rather than potato vodka) is better for this unusual Martini.

Because Kina Lillet no longer exists, Lillet Blanc must once again serve as a substitute. Also, the gin in Fleming's era would have been of a stronger proof (Gordon's gin is no longer as strong as it was), so a 47% ABV London Dry, or higher, is the best choice here, as well as a vodka distilled from grain.

GLASSWARE: Champagne coupe
GARNISH: Lemon twist

- **3 oz. dry gin**
- **1 oz. vodka**
- **½ oz. Lillet Blanc**

1. Add all of the ingredients to a cocktail shaker filled with ice, shake vigorously until chilled, and strain into the champagne coupe.

2. Garnish with the lemon twist.

- ESPRESSO MARTINI -

This is possibly the best-known creation from the legendary Dick Bradsell, who almost single-handedly revived London's cocktail scene in the 1980s. Originally titled the Vodka Espresso, it was created in 1983 when a customer (possibly a famous model) asked for something to "wake me up, and f*ck me up." After further tinkering, it later was rechristened the Espresso Martini. Eventually, it transformed into another drink Bradsell served, the Pharmaceutical Stimulant, when he opened the bar Pharmacy in 1998.

Even if it will cool in the shaker, be sure to use a steaming hot shot of espresso so that the cocktail retains the crema.

GLASSWARE: Cocktail glass
GARNISH: 3 coffee beans

- 2 oz. vodka
- 1 oz. freshly brewed espresso
- ½ oz. coffee liqueur

- 1 teaspoon Simple Syrup (optional, see page 24)

1. Chill a cocktail glass.

2. Add the ingredients to a cocktail shaker filled with ice, shake vigorously until chilled, and double-strain into the chilled glass.

3. Garnish with three coffee beans placed closely together.

- BRAMBLE -

Another Dick Bradsell invention, this one coming during his tenure at Fred's Club in Soho. The Bramble is the fruit of his quest to create a truly British drink. In Bradsell's words, it resembles a "gin sour with blackberry stuff in it." He even suggests a variation where the crème de mure is replaced with Ribena, a cheap black currant concentrate.

Be sure to use crushed ice (an important detail). For the garnish, either a raspberry or a blackberry works. When he first made the drink, Bradsell originally used a raspberry because he had no blackberries available, though he eventually swapped them in.

GLASSWARE: Rocks glass
GARNISH: Raspberry or blackberry

- 2 oz. gin
- 1 oz. fresh lemon juice
- ½ oz. Simple Syrup (see page 24)
- ½ oz. crème de mure, to top

1. Add all of the ingredients, except the crème de mure, to a cocktail shaker filled with ice, shake vigorously until chilled, and strain into a rocks glass filled with crushed ice.

2. Lace the crème de mure on top of the drink and garnish with a blackberry or raspberry.

- THE BREAKFAST MARTINI -

Salvatore Calabrese, the longtime president of the United Kingdom Bartender's Guild, was originally inspired to create this "marmalade cocktail" in 2000, after being forced by his English wife, Sue, to have marmalade on toast for breakfast (he normally just drinks a cup of coffee) the day after a particularly tough shift. Inspired by the flavor of the marmalade, he created the Breakfast Martini when he went to work at London's Library Bar in the Lanesborough Hotel later that day, and it has since inspired bartenders all over the world to create their own takes on it. Make sure you use a high-quality preserve to really make the drink shine.

GLASSWARE: Cocktail glass
GARNISH: Grated orange zest

- 1¾ oz. gin
- ½ oz. Cointreau
- ½ oz. fresh lemon juice
- 1 bar spoon fine-cut orange marmalade

1. Chill the cocktail glass.

2. Add the ingredients to cocktail shaker and stir until the marmalade has emulsified.

3. Add ice and shake vigorously until chilled.

4. Strain into the chilled cocktail glass.

5. Grate some orange zest over the cocktail.

THE WEST END

CUBISM • MITCHER'S AND PEAR • PRIDE •
VERA LYNN • MIRAFLORES NEGRONI •
GIN LANE • ROSE BLOSSOM • SGROPPINO
PLAGIATO • VESCA NEGRONI • FALLEN
MADONNA • DORSET DONKEY • LADY IN RED •
PERSEPHONE • LONDON CALLING • CRESTING
THE SUMMIT • WICCA CAULDRON CURE • HAY
ZEUS • YINCHUAN • NEWTON PUNCH • FIRE
STAR PUNCH • VITAMIN SEA • #1 HIGH C
SPRITZ • BASILICO • FIZZ KAFFIR • JAPANESE
WHISPERS • THE BLACK LEAF • SPEEDY
GONZALES • LEMONGRASS MOJITO •
BLENDED UNION • DARKNESS AND DISGRACE

The West End of London is among the world's most famous urban areas. Centered around the iconic Trafalgar Square, it bustles with countless sumptuous theaters and some of the planet's most luxurious hotels. Endless hordes of locals and tourists eagerly take in everything the West End has to offer.

Appropriately, a number of the world's best-known cocktails were born here. In the 1840s, celebrity chef Alexis Soyer created what might be the first blue drinks and jello shots at the Reform Club just off Trafalgar Square. Hotel bars here began serving drinks of the highest quality in the 19th century, and are still going strong today.

The West End was also the epicenter of London's cocktail rebirth that started in the '80s and exploded in the '90s, with Dick Bradsell's pioneering work spreading across the bars and clubs of the quarter at a time when cocktails were still considered rather tawdry in the rest of the city.

Today, high-quality cocktail bars are literally everywhere in the West End. These are just a few. Some are well-known and take pride of place among the best bars in the world; others are looking to make their name in a fiercely competitive and expensive neighborhood in a fiercely competitive and expensive city.

100 WARDOUR STREET

100 WARDOUR STREET, SOHO
LONDON W1F 0TN

– CUBISM –

Named after the artwork of a father of Cubism, Pablo Picasso, this drink designed by Quaglino's head mixologist Federico Pasian is a twist on an Old Fashioned, using four liquors (rum, Cognac, bourbon, and Fernet-Branca Menta) as the base to reflect the four sides of a square, in addition to the four drops of cherry gelatin that grace the side of the glass.

GLASSWARE: Rocks glass
GARNISH: 4 drops cherry gelatin

- 1 oz. Bulleit Bourbon
- 2 teaspoons Cognac
- 2 teaspoons Diplomatico Reserva Rum
- 2 teaspoons Simple Syrup (see page 24)
- 1 teaspoon Fernet-Branca Menta
- 1 strip lemon zest

1. Add all of the ingredients to a mixing glass filled with ice and stir until chilled.

2. Strain into a rocks glass containing a large block of ice.

3. Apply the four drops of cherry gelatin just below the rim of the glass, making sure they are parallel to the rim.

– MICHTER'S AND PEAR –

An incredibly simple drink to make, bar manager Anna Sebastian's fusion of an Old Fashioned and a Gimlet provides a zingy and irresistible combination thanks to the pear cordial and the bourbon, which, despite the name, doesn't have to be Michter's.

GLASSWARE: Coupette

GARNISH: None

- 1¼ oz. pear cordial
- 1½ oz. bourbon
- 2 dashes salt

1. Place a large ice cube in the coupette.

2. Add the ingredients and stir until chilled.

ARTESIAN AT THE LANGHAM

When she joined the Artesian team in 2017, bar manager Anna Sebastian had big shoes to fill. Former heads Alex Kratena (who has since opened Tayēr + Elementary, see pages 306–307) and Simone Caporale had helmed an operation repeatedly listed #1 at the World's 50 Best Bars before moving on to new challenges.

It was a big job for a woman who "accidentally" fell into her hospitality career: "I was on a completely different career path when I left school, about to join the military," she explains. "I see a lot of similarities between the two. The structure, consistency, but most importantly the camaraderie and sister/brotherhood of working so closely together, like a well-oiled machine."

Sebastian won extensive praise for her work prior to her arrival at Artesian, particularly at the impressive Beaufort Bar in The Savoy. She now oversees a brand-new cocktail program that aims to create simple cocktails using lab-based preparation methods: "At the bar, we play with the idea that 'less can be more,' taking two key ingredients and extracting flavor in a different way through use of equipment that we have in our lab downstairs. We think a drink should always make people ask a question."

That simplicity, however, is served up in an opulent package. Massive chandeliers and leather furniture create a polished, well-heeled atmosphere. Nestled in the luxurious Langham hotel, the combination of elegance and simplicity creates a truly special London drinks experience, and a welcome new chapter in the Artesian's history.

THE BAPTIST BAR AT L'OSCAR

2-6, SOUTHAMPTON ROW, HOLBORN
LONDON WC1B 4AA

- PRIDE -

The Pride is inspired by Oscar Wilde's two favorite drinks, absinthe and Champagne. The combination of the Jasmine Tea-Infused Vodka and the star anise extract recalls the aroma of absinthe, an element that is balanced by the freshness and citrus of the Lime & Sage Sherbet. The result, which was dreamed up by bar manager Luca Rapetti, is a refreshing and fizzy Champagne cocktail that you can enjoy any time of day.

GLASSWARE: Retro Fizzio 1910 or coupe
GARNISH: Strip from 1 page of *The Picture of Dorian Gray*

- 1 oz. Jasmine Tea-Infused Vodka (Baptist uses Ketel One)
- 1 oz. Lime & Sage Sherbet
- Vignoble Guillaume Flûte Enchantée sparkling wine, to top
- Star anise extract, to mist

1. Place the vodka and sherbet in a cocktail shaker filled with ice and shake vigorously until chilled.

2. Strain into the chosen glass and top with the sparkling wine.

3. Spray the star anise extract on top and tie the page strip to the glass's stem.

JASMINE TEA-INFUSED VODKA: Place a 750 ml bottle of vodka and 3 tablespoons of jasmine pearl tea in a mason jar and let steep for 3 to 4 hours. Strain before using or storing.

LIME & SAGE SHERBET: Place 11 oz. fresh lime juice and 21 oz. caster sugar in a saucepan and bring to a simmer, stirring until the sugar has dissolved. Add 1½ oz. chopped lime peel and 1½ oz. sage (leaves and stems), cook for 5 minutes, and remove the pan from heat. When it has cooled, pour the mixture into a vacuum bag and vacuum seal it. Let the mixture steep for 4 hours, strain, and pour back into the bag. Vacuum seal again and store in the refrigerator for up to 1 week.

BAR BANTER
LUCA RAPETTI
BAR MANAGER, THE BAPTIST BAR

Walking into the Baptist Bar feels like discovering a London secret. With a two-story, high-ceilinged design and indulgent, purple-and-gold decorations, it seems a venue that was made for Liberace. (The second floor is the hotel's restaurant, the Baptist Grill.) Bar manager Luca Rapetti, who has worked at London's leading hotel bars, has overseen Baptist's drinks offerings since it opened.

THIS IS A UNIQUE VENUE. TELL US MORE ABOUT IT.
This hotel is different from many others. It's a boutique hotel, but we aim to deliver not only a high standard of service. We're also aiming for something bohemian and flamboyant. The design of the bar is very much French Belle Epoque and the designer, Jacques Garcia, is French and known for this style.

We wanted a bar that was different from bars in the area as there are a few hotels here, but they cater to people working in the area, groups from law firms and finance offices coming in after work. Here we wanted to create a place that aims for simple quality of drinks and a cozy atmosphere.

HOW DID YOU SHAPE YOUR COCKTAIL MENU?
I remember that when we were developing the menu for the bar the contractors were still working away, drilling and knocking down walls. We've only been open for just over a year but we've already achieved great things and this location, a former Baptist church, has a great history and design in an area that's full of history as well. It's a great place to work.

Our menu has stayed the same since the beginning so we can show people what we can do, and we gave it a biblical theme as we felt that made sense given the venue. We are also drawing on the legacy of Oscar Wilde, after whom the hotel is named. We use as a motto one of his lines: "Every saint has a past and every sinner has a future." When you look at our menu, our Old Testament–themed side is the saint's side, and our New Testament–themed side is the "sinner" side. That idea is important for us.

WHAT HAS APPEALED TO YOU ABOUT WORKING IN HOTEL BARS AND DEVELOPING YOUR CAREER IN THIS SPECIFIC FIELD?

I'm focused on standards and really like working in a consistent way. I also really think that guest interaction and service, creating tailor-made service, is the most important thing at hotel bars. I really think the cocktail is only around 30 to 40 percent of the overall guest experience.

You obviously can find this in other bars, but I think that in London, hotels are the best place for this mentality, and to train and develop yourself in this specific direction. Standards, values, and procedures become the pillars of your service while you need to adapt yourself flexibly for the individual guests you work with. In a luxury boutique hotel, where guests are paying a lot of money, it also means that everything needs to be done right. This is the kind of environment I wanted to be in and what originally inspired me when I started my career.

CAHOOTS

13 KINGLY COURT
SOHO, LONDON W1B 5PW

– VERA LYNN –

Cahoots' most popular cocktail is named after the iconic singer who was a household name during World War II. Bar manager Michele Venturini authored this tribute to Lynn's legacy, which is intensely fruity, with strong flavors of apple and elderflower, but isn't too sweet thanks to the acidity of the lime juice and spice of the ginger in the puree. By the end of the drink you'll be humming Lynn's bittersweet anthem, "We'll Meet Again."

GLASSWARE: Vera Lynn mug or highball glass
GARNISH: Dehydrated apple slice, mint sprig, and cherry apple

- 1⅜ oz. Tanqueray No. 10 gin
- 1¾ oz. fresh apple juice
- 1⅜ oz. Pear & Ginger Puree
- 2 teaspoons Bottlegreen Elderflower Cordial
- ½ oz. fresh lime juice
- 1 dash black pepper

1. Place all of the ingredients in a cocktail shaker filled with ice and shake vigorously until chilled.

2. Strain into the Vera Lynn mug or highball glass.

3. Garnish with the dehydrated apple slice, sprig of mint, and cherry apple.

PEAR & GINGER PUREE (ADJUST AMOUNTS AS NEEDED): Place 10 pears, 1¾ oz. chopped fresh ginger, 1 bottle of Bottlegreen Lemongrass Cordial, and 1 tablespoon freshly ground pepper in a blender and puree until smooth.

CEVICHE

17 FRITH STREET, SOHO, LONDON W1D 4RG

It's no longer impossible to find Peruvian-themed restaurants and bars in most cosmopolitan cities. One of the first to spot the trend was British Peruvian Martin Morales, who founded Ceviche in 2012: "I've been cooking since I was nine and learned Peruvian recipes from my great aunts in Lima and my grandmother in the Andes," Morales says. "I could see a wave of Peruvian cuisine growing and I wanted to be a leading voice in that movement, as I wish to ensure that tradition and authenticity are upheld—and that our food and ingredient stories are told legitimately."

Combine Martin's dedication to showcasing Peru's magic with his extensive experience in hospitality and *eso es todo*—a winning recipe that serves up phenomenal food and drinks. His success is confirmed by the subsequent opening of another Ceviche on Old Street and the Andina restaurants, which also serve Andean-inspired food.

Of course, this makes Ceviche the perfect place in London to sample an excellent Pisco Sour, as well as many other pisco cocktails. In addition to food and drinks, Ceviche also has its own record label, Tiger's Milk Records, which promotes Peruvian culture.

Regarding Ceviche's central motto, *"Aqui se cocina con cariño,"* Morales said, "It means 'Here we cook with love.' That describes not only the way we cook but also the way we treat and work with our customers; the way we source our ingredients and work with suppliers; and in the way we manage sustainability and our social and environmental impact."

A cocktail from a Peruvian restaurant in London must include pisco. So here's a unique take on the Negroni, the choice of hipsters everywhere these days. The rhubarb-spiked gin pokes through, adding a little extra sweetness.

GLASSWARE: Rocks glass
GARNISH: Thin slice of rhubarb

- **2 teaspoons Whitley Neill Rhubarb & Ginger Gin**
- **2 teaspoons La Diablada Acholado Pisco**
- **¾ oz. Contratto Bitter liqueur**
- **¾ oz. Belsazar Rose Vermouth**

1. Add all of the ingredients to a mixing glass filled with ice and stir until chilled.

2. Strain into a rocks glass filled with ice.

3. Garnish with the thin slice of rhubarb.

THE CORAL ROOM AT THE BLOOMSBURY HOTEL

16-22 GREAT RUSSELL STREET
BLOOMSBURY
LONDON WC1B 3NN

- GIN LANE -

Gin Lane is named after the famous mid-18th century William Hogarth print (see page 9) that pins the collapse of British society on the consumption of gin. This drink is softly sweet, tangy, and elegant thanks to the deft touch of general manager Giovanni Spezziga. The combination of the elderflower liqueur and rose syrup lends the descent into anarchy a flowery bouquet.

GLASSWARE: Cocktail glass
GARNISH: Dehydrated rosebud

- 1¾ oz. Viognier
- 1 oz. Hendrick's Gin
- 2 teaspoons St-Germain
- 2 teaspoons Monin Rose Syrup
- 1 teaspoon agave nectar

1. Chill the cocktail glass.

2. Add all of the ingredients to a mixing glass filled with ice and stir until chilled.

3. Strain into the chilled glass and garnish with the dehydrated rosebud.

- ROSE BLOSSOM -

Don't be fooled by the pink glitter; there's a lot of depth here. The gin imparts a little punch; the Italicus brings earthy, herbal goodness; the elderflower cordial adds something fragrant, and the sparkling wine makes it really refreshing. Another stunning offering from the mind of Spezziga.

GLASSWARE: Coupette
GARNISH: Edible pink glitter

- 2 teaspoons Tanqueray No. 10 gin
- 1¼ oz. Italicus Rosolio di Bergamotto liqueur
- 2 teaspoons Bottlegreen Elderflower Cordial
- 3 dashes Peychaud's Bitters
- Sparkling wine, to top

1. Chill the coupette.

2. Add all of the ingredients, except the sparkling wine, to a mixing glass filled with ice and stir until chilled.

3. Place a small block of ice in the chilled coupette and double-strain the cocktail over the ice.

4. Top with the sparkling wine and sprinkle edible pink glitter over the top.

- SGROPPINO PLAGIATO -

A collaboration between Fitz's head bartender Morten Kjaerulff and Kimpton Fitzroy's pastry chef, Thibault Marchand, resulted in this refreshing serve. What better way to celebrate the miracle of homemade sorbet than with sparkling wine, after all?

GLASSWARE: Goblet

GARNISH: Flower of choice

- 1 scoop Tropical Fruit Sorbet
- 1¾ oz. Select Aperitivo
- Prosecco, to top

1. Place the scoop of sorbet in the goblet.

2. Pour the Select Aperitivo over the sorbet and top with the Prosecco.

3. Garnish with a flower and serve with a spoon.

TROPICAL FRUIT SORBET: Place 3½ oz. water, 3½ oz. sugar, and ½ oz. fresh lemon juice in a saucepan and bring to a simmer, stirring until the sugar has dissolved. Add the seeds of 1 vanilla bean, 14 oz. mango puree, and 3½ oz. passion fruit puree and stir until combined. Freeze for 24 hours and let sit at room temperature for 5 or 10 minutes before serving. Churn the mixture in an ice cream maker if a smoother consistency is desired.

The first reason behind the success of this drink is the high quality of the ingredients used in this Kjaerulff–helmed concoction. The second is the "Vesca Ice." This is the only cocktail in this book that requires a degree of preparation with the ice used, but the result is a truly unique Negroni.

GLASSWARE: Rocks glass
GARNISH: Lime twist

- 1 oz. Dolin Blanc Vermouth
- 1 oz. Luxardo Bitter Bianco
- 1 oz. Fords Gin
- 1 block Vesca Ice

1. Add the vermouth, Luxardo, and gin to a mixing glass filled with ice and stir until chilled.

2. Strain over a block of Vesca Ice into a rocks glass.

3. Garnish with the lime twist.

VESCA ICE (ADJUST AMOUNTS AS NEEDED): Add 3½ quarts water, 35 oz. aloe vera juice, 17½ oz. strained woodland strawberry juice, 17½ oz. Sacred Rosehip Cup aperitif, 15 drops MSK Coconut Flavouring Compound, and, if desired, ½ oz. red food coloring to a large mixing bowl, stir to combine, and freeze until solid, about 72 hours. Cut into smaller blocks that will fit into a rocks glass.

HIDE BELOW

85 PICCADILLY, MAYFAIR, LONDON W1J 7NB

You could be forgiven for thinking that HIDE is nothing more than a fancy, Michelin-starred restaurant on Piccadilly. However, sneak downstairs to HIDE Below and you step into a spirits wonderland. HIDE Below boasts top-class wine (celebrated wine merchant Hedonism is a partner), whisky, spirits, and private booths, as well as exceptional cocktails.

It is the latest brainchild of bar manager Oskar Kinberg, who moved to London in 2005 to "take a year out" and make some money working in a bar: "That year still hasn't stopped. I quickly found myself loving what I was doing and decided to stay in this industry and make a career out of it."

The latest step in that career is sumptuously decorated, starting with the stunning, winding wooden staircase that leads to HIDE Below's classy den. Wood paneling and tasteful lighting impart a warm, intimate glow, a welcome contrast to the busy and deafening chaos of Piccadilly.

How does Kinberg approach HIDE Below's cocktail menu? "I usually start with one ingredient and add others to make it taste as good as possible," he says. "The last thing I do is remove anything that is superfluous and doesn't come through. If it says 'strawberries and cream' on the menu, that's what it should taste like. Not sandalwood and musk."

He's also not afraid to incorporate unusual ingredients to add an exotic angle to his drinks (just take a look at the Fallen Madonna on the next page). Reviewers routinely praise the quality of these cocktails, not least for Kinberg's common-sense approach: "The key is to make them tasty," he insists. "Sometimes it starts with a fruit and sometimes a spirit. Regardless of method and ingredients, the end result must be very tasty."

- FALLEN MADONNA -

If there's aloe vera in it, that makes it healthy, right? The Fallen Madonna is sweet and straightforward, and the aloe provides a silken texture. While the use of flat tonic may seem controversial, there's only one way to find out if you agree with bar manager Oskar Kinberg's choice to employ it.

GLASSWARE: Toyo Old Fashioned glass
GARNISH: Pea shoots and flowers

- 1¾ oz. Tanqueray gin
- 1¼ oz. flat tonic water
- 2 teaspoons fresh lemon juice
- 1¾ teaspoons Simple Syrup (see page 24)
- ⅞ oz. aloe vera

1. Add all of the ingredients to a cocktail shaker filled with ice and shake vigorously until chilled.

2. Strain into a Toyo Old Fashioned glass filled with ice cubes.

3. Garnish with pea shoots and flowers.

HIX

66-70 BREWER STREET, SOHO
LONDON W1F 9UP

- DORSET DONKEY -

This very British take on the Moscow Mule comes via Dustin MacMillan. For the garnish, HIX swaps between fresh seasonal blueberries in the summer, blackberries in autumn, and Morello cherries preserved in apple eau de vie in colder months. Feel free to go with your own seasonal variation depending on where you live.

GLASSWARE: Highball glass
GARNISH: 2 sage leaves and either a seasonal berry
or a Morello cherry

- 1¾ oz. Black Cow Vodka
- 1¾ teaspoons Morello cherry liquid
- ½ oz. fresh lime juice
- FeverTree Ginger Ale, to top

1. Add all of the ingredients, except the ginger ale, to the highball glass and fill it with ice cubes. Stir for a few seconds to combine.

2. Top with the ginger ale and stir to incorporate.

3. Garnish with the sage leaves and either an appropriate seasonal berry or a Morello cherry.

- LADY IN RED -

This cocktail is inspired by the Negroni Sbagliato, with a floral and fruity finish. It is an excellent representative of what cocktails in London are all about: creativity, provenance, and international connections. In this case, here's an Italian-inspired drink with a twist created by a French mixologist (lead bartender Lucas Brun), utilizing a few English-based ingredients and being served up in a true London institution.

GLASSWARE: Coupette

GARNISH: None

- ¾ oz. London Dry gin
- ½ oz. Campari
- ¼ oz. Strawberry Vinegar
- 2⅛ oz. Ridgeview English sparkling wine

1. Add all of the ingredients to a mixing glass filled with ice and stir until chilled.

2. Strain into a coupette containing a block of ice.

STRAWBERRY VINEGAR (MAKES 1 ¹/₃ QUARTS): Place 10½ oz. fresh strawberries, 26 oz. apple cider vinegar, 2 whole lemons, 1 teaspoon grenadine, and 1½ oz. Simple Syrup (see page 24) in a vacuum bag, vacuum seal it, and let it sit for 3 days. Strain, taste to see if it is sweet enough, and add more sugar if necessary.

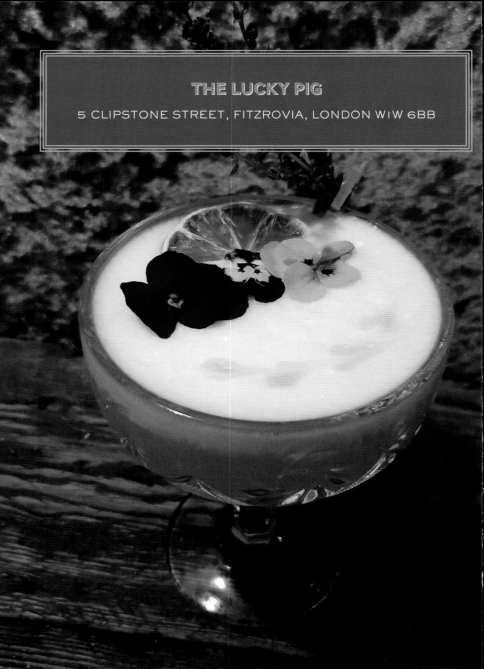

- PERSEPHONE -

Made in honor of the Greek goddess Persephone, queen of the underworld—Lucky Pig is located in a basement—and the goddess of spring and nature, this is a refreshing drink that head bartender Konrad Stemplewski designed with spring in his native Poland in mind.

GLASSWARE: Coupe

GARNISH: Dehydrated lime slice, edible flowers, lemon thyme sprig, and lavender sprig

- 1 slice cucumber
- 1 slice fresh ginger
- 4 to 5 mint leaves
- 1⅜ oz. No.3 London Dry Gin
- ½ oz. St-Germain
- 1⅜ oz. apple juice
- ½ oz. Fortunella Golden Orange liqueur
- ¾ oz. fresh lime juice
- ¾ oz. Lavender Syrup
- 1 egg white
- 4 dashes lavender bitters, to top

1. Place the cucumber slice, ginger slice, and mint leaves in a cocktail shaker and gently muddle.

2. Add ice and the remaining ingredients, except for the lavender bitters, and shake vigorously until chilled.

3. Double-strain into the coupe. Top with the lavender bitters and garnish with the dehydrated lime slice, edible flowers, and sprigs of lemon thyme and lavender.

LAVENDER SYRUP: Add 3 parts sugar, 2 parts water, and a generous handful of lavender to a saucepan and warm over medium heat, stirring until the sugar has dissolved. Remove from heat, let cool completely, and strain before using or storing.

MILK & HONEY

61 POLAND STREET, SOHO
LONDON W1F 7NU

– LONDON CALLING –

Chris Jepson's simple and classy variation on a Gin Sour is the only cocktail that has stayed on the Milk & Honey cocktail menu since it was created in 2002, a testament to how good it is.

GLASSWARE: Coupe

GARNISH: Grapefruit twist

- 1¾ oz. gin
- ⅜ oz. Tio Pepe Fino Sherry
- ½ oz. fresh lemon juice
- ½ oz. Simple Syrup (see page 24)
- 2 dashes orange bitters

1. Add all of the ingredients to a cocktail shaker filled with ice and shake vigorously until chilled.

2. Strain into the coupe.

3. Garnish with the grapefruit twist.

BAR BANTER
PIERRE-MARIE BISSON
MANAGER, MILK & HONEY

A member's club now 18 years old, Milk & Honey began in New York, founded by the legendary bartender Sasha Petraske, who then opened the London branch in 2002. Though Petraske passed away in 2015, the venue is still going strong. Pierre-Marie Bisson has been running the club for four years, and it remains a London institution.

HOW HAVE DRINKS AT THE CLUB CHANGED IN YOUR TIME HERE?
I've seen things evolve from a point where, let's say, there was maybe a little lack of interest from customers—2015 was a good year for homemade ingredients and scientific methods, but the more classic cocktails were being left behind.

You could see a change happening. People are going back to classics and even the big brands at competitions would tell you "no more than five ingredients. You can only use one homemade ingredient and we need to be able to recreate it."

WHAT DOES IT TAKE TO BE A GOOD BARTENDER IN LONDON?
Early in my career, I fell into the trap that some guys fall into who've done serious bar work. One time, I gave myself a break for a minute and my manager comes around and asks what I'm doing. I said, "Oh, I'm taking a minute, everything is done." Never, ever, say that to anyone who has more experience than you, because it's never true. She immediately slammed me on a million details that I hadn't covered and I realized that she was right.

It's great to learn how to do bartending in a place that's really busy because it means you learn to be fast and you learn to be efficient. Then, you've learned how to be an efficient technician, if not necessar-

ily a true "bartender." It's incredibly valuable experience that will take you to the next level.

HOW HAVE THINGS CHANGED HERE SINCE YOU BEGAN MANAGING THE PLACE, AND WHAT ARE YOU MOST PROUD OF IN YOUR TIME HERE?

This is a members' club. So the thing that I'm most proud of is the rapport that I get to build with our guests and regulars, getting to know them, what they like to drink, and building that trust. It also means that you can interact better with them and also make recommendations that you think they might enjoy while they also understand that you're not trying to sell them something.

Sasha Petraske would say, "Give me someone for half an hour and I'll teach them how to make a perfect Martini." But that's not what service is about. That's just about making a good drink. It's about going into the freezer and stretching your back out a bit to get that glass that's extra cold at the back. It's being able to smile at the end of a busy shift and still make that last drink for that last order at the same quality that you were making at the beginning of the night. It's about transforming a "no" into a solution. It's about getting the details right.

- CRESTING THE SUMMIT -

Here's a fun fact: Mr. Fogg's and Metaxa were two of the sponsors for the world's highest-ever dinner party, held on Mount Everest in 2018. Simone Spagnoli's inspiration for this cocktail was the butter tea popular amongst sherpas, called "su cha" by them and "pocha" in the rest of China. It is a very common drink in Nepal, Bhutan, India, and China (the tea, not the cocktail).

GLASSWARE: Thermos flask
GARNISH: Confectioners' sugar

- 1½ oz. Metaxa
- 2½ oz. Spiced Tea Cordial
- ⅛ oz. yogurt powder

1. Ideally, this drink is prepared in a large batch so feel free to adjust the proportions as needed. Add all of the ingredients to an appropriately sized container and give it a little shake to incorporate the yogurt powder.

2. Pour each cocktail into a Thermos flask and garnish with confectioners' sugar (representing snow) on the side.

SPICED TEA CORDIAL (MAKES 35 OZ., ADJUST AMOUNTS AS NEEDED): Place 35 oz. boiling water, 7 oz. sugar, and 10 bags of English breakfast tea in a container and steep for 2 minutes, stirring gently a few times. Remove the tea bags, place the tea in a saucepan, add 10 star anise pods, 15 whole cloves, 3 cinnamon sticks, and 1¾ oz. unsalted butter, and cook over low heat until the flavor is to your liking, about 30 to 35 minutes. Strain through cheesecloth before using or storing.

Celtic Druids and the ancient pagan rituals in England provide the inspiration for this brew, especially with the use of rhubarb, a common British ingredient that is known for its medicinal properties. The best feature of this potion created by Alberto Ceronne and Valerio Paternostro, however, is that the color will start changing after you've taken the first few sips.

GLASSWARE: Custom cauldron glass or snifter
GARNISH: 1 teaspoon pea flower extract or oil-based blue food coloring

- 1½ oz. Triple Citrus-Infused Bosford Rose Gin
- ⅞ oz. fresh lemon juice
- ⅞ oz. Bottlegreen Rhubarb & Ginger Cordial
- 1 teaspoon Ginger Syrup
- 1 oz. Moet & Chandon Champagne, to top

1. Add all of the ingredients, except for the Champagne, to a cocktail shaker filled with ice and shake vigorously until chilled.

2. Double-strain over ice into the chosen glass and top with the Champagne.

3. Just before serving, dash the pea flower extract over the top and serve without stirring.

TRIPLE CITRUS-INFUSED BOSFORD ROSE GIN (ADJUST AMOUNTS AS NEEDED): Place the whole peels of a lemon, orange, and a grapefruit and a 750 ml bottle of Bosford Rose Gin into a vacuum bag and cook sous vide at 152°F for 2 hours. Strain the liquid back into the bottle. If you do not have access to a sous vide, place the bottle of gin in a mason jar and add the citrus peels. Let steep for 24 hours before straining back into the bottle.

GINGER SYRUP: Take a 2-inch piece of ginger and chop it. Add it to a standard Simple Syrup (see page 24) while the mixture is simmering, remove from heat, and let cool. Remove the ginger before using or storing.

– HAY ZEUS –

The original goal of this cocktail was to create a tasty, well-balanced, and blue Margarita. That charge inspired general manager Luke Condell to create a special cordial for the occasion: "For me, it was all about highlighting those grassy, green, and vegetal vibes you get from highland tequila and mezcals, which then led to the creation of Zeus Juice."

GLASSWARE: Ceramic white bowl
GARNISH: Cornflower leaves

- ½ oz. Olmeca Altos Tequila Plata
- ½ oz. fresh lime juice
- 1¾ oz. Zeus Juice Cordial

1. Add all of the ingredients to a cocktail shaker filled with ice and shake vigorously until chilled.

2. Strain into a ceramic white bowl containing a block of ice.

3. Garnish with the cornflower leaves.

ZEUS JUICE CORDIAL (MAKES 2½ CUPS): Place ⅜ oz. crushed hay, 5¼ oz. celery juice, and 3½ oz. caster sugar in a blender and blitz until combined. Strain through cheesecloth and stir in ⅞ oz. Simple Syrup (see page 24), 8 oz. Mezcal Amores, 3½ oz. blue wine (Gik is a trusted brand), ½ oz. saline solution (small pinch of salt mixed with water), and 2 drops of MSK Toasted Coconut Flavour Drops. Use immediately or store in an airtight container. The cordial will keep in the refrigerator for up to 2 weeks.

PEONY BAR IN THE OPIUM COCKTAIL AND DIM SUM PARLOUR

15-16 GERRARD STREET, LONDON W1D 6JE

Opium has been serving top-quality, delicious drinks in the heart of London's Chinatown since 2012. The door is so undistinguished that you have to look *really* hard to spot it. Once inside, though, there is a lot to explore.

Co-founded by London legend Dre Masso and bar entrepreneur Eric Yu, the bar owes its selection of Asian-themed cocktails to a Parisian. General manager Jeremy Pascal transitioned from working at high-end restaurants to bar work and hasn't looked back since. "This is a den of Oriental eclecticism," Pascal says. "Opium transports you back to 1920s Shanghai with sprawling corridors and hidden booths. It's composed of three bars spread over three floors: the Apothecary, Peony, and Academy, where we offer three distinctive menus for an unforgettable journey."

A mouthwatering dim sum menu is available across the entire facility, too.

Among Pascal's major challenges: keep things varied and interesting with separate, themed menus in each of Opium's bars. "We do tend to work on themed cocktail menus, which guides us to a route to take regarding influences and inspiration," he says.

The Academy bar aims at creating drinks that complement Asian cooking. The Peony focuses on the history and flavors of Chinese cities. Finally, the Apothecary serves its drinks from little medicine jars, with labels written in Cantonese and flavors inspired by Chinese and Southeast Asian medicine.

– YINCHUAN –

nspired by the local market in the Chinese city of Yinchuan, general manager Jeremy Pascal's creation is one of the signature cocktails from a bar located in the heart of London's Chinatown. Known for producing rice, cereals, and oils, Yinchuan enjoys beautiful natural scenery and favorable conditions for agriculture.

GLASSWARE: Rocks glass
GARNISH: Sesame cracker and (optional) edible butterfly

- 1⅜ oz Fat-Washed Ragtime Rye Whiskey
- ¾ oz. red date tea
- 1 teaspoon Sichuan Peppercorn Syrup
- 1 teaspoon crème de peche
- 3 drops vanilla bitters
- Hay, for smoke gun

1. Place all of the ingredients, except for the hay, in a mixing glass filled with ice and stir until chilled.

2. Strain into a rocks glass filled with whiskey stones or other frozen stones.

3. Using a smoke gun filled with hay, smoke the cocktail for 10 to 15 seconds.

4. Garnish with a sesame cracker and, if desired, an edible butterfly.

FAT-WASHED RAGTIME RYE WHISKEY: Place 1⅞ oz. sesame oil and a 750 ml bottle of Ragtime Rye in a container, shake vigorously, and store in a cool, dry place for 24 hours. Freeze the mixture until the oil solidifies into a solid layer. Remove the oil and strain the whiskey through cheesecloth before using or storing.

SICHUAN PEPPERCORN SYRUP (MAKES APPROXIMATELY 1½ CUPS): Place 9 oz. water, 9 oz. honey, and ¾ oz. Sichuan peppercorns in a vacuum bag and sous vide for 6 hours at 120°F. Strain before using or storing. If you do not have access to a sous vide, place all of the ingredients in a saucepan and bring to a boil. Reduce heat and let the mixture simmer for 20 minutes. Remove from heat, let cool, and strain before using or storing.

- NEWTON PUNCH -

Simone De Luca took his inspiration for this punch from the concept of aether, which was used in various gravitational theories centuries ago as a medium that would explain gravitation and what causes it, including in one of Sir Isaac Newton's first published theories of gravitation, *Philosophiæ Naturalis Principia Mathematica*. In that text, Newton based the description of planetary motions on a theoretical law of dynamic interactions. In this homage, the equal proportions of the ingredients manage to create a perfect balance through their interaction.

GLASSWARE: Rocks glass

GARNISH: Apple blossom

- 1 oz. 30&40 Double Jus Aperitif de Normandie
- 1 oz. Somerset Cider Brandy
- 1 oz. Briottet Manzana Verde
- 1 oz. Apple & Tea Cordial
- 1 oz. Curious Apple Cider
- 1 oz. fresh lemon juice
- 1 oz. unfiltered apple juice

1. Add all of the ingredients to a mixing glass filled with ice. Using another mixing glass, utilize the Cuban roll method (see page 104) to mix the cocktail.

2. Strain into a rocks glass containing a block of ice.

3. Garnish with an apple blossom.

APPLE & TEA CORDIAL: Place 14 oz. apple juice, 7 oz. brewed Earl Grey tea, and 28 oz. sugar in a saucepan and bring to a boil. Reduce heat to low and simmer, while stirring, until the sugar has dissolved, about 10 minutes. Stir in ⅜ oz. citric acid, remove the mixture from heat, and let cool completely before using or storing.

- FIRE STAR PUNCH -

This serve is inspired by the planet Mars, which is known as the "Fire Star" in Asian cultures. Senior bartender Davide Leanza used ingredients that would be eaten by astronauts (as determined by NASA) if they were to go to Mars—corn and red bell peppers would definitely be in the diet. The aperitif-related ingredients are a nod to the Italian astronomer Giovanni Schiaparelli, who helped produce the first detailed map of Mars.

GLASSWARE: Goblet
GARNISH: Baby corn and cornflower

- ⅞ oz. mellow corn whiskey
- ⅞ oz. Wild Turkey Rye Whiskey
- ¾ oz. Martini & Rossi Riserva Speciale Rubino
- ½ oz. Martini & Rossi Bitter
- 1⅛ oz. brewed hibiscus tea
- ½ oz. Red Pepper Syrup
- ½ oz. Citric Acid Solution

1. Add all of the ingredients to a mixing glass filled with ice. Using another mixing glass, pour the cocktail back and forth between the glasses three times; the more distance between your glasses, the better. This method of mixing is known as the "Cuban roll."

2. Strain the cocktail into a goblet containing a block of ice.

3. Garnish with the baby corn and cornflower.

RED PEPPER SYRUP: Place 2 seeded and chopped red bell peppers, 9 oz. water, and 17½ oz. caster sugar in a saucepan and bring to a boil. Reduce heat and let simmer, while stirring, until the sugar has dissolved, 5 to 10 minutes. Remove from heat, let cool, and then pour the mixture into a mason jar without straining it. Refrigerate overnight and strain the mixture before using or storing.

CITRIC ACID SOLUTION: Place 35 oz. water and 2 oz. citric acid in a container and stir until the citric acid has dissolved.

– VITAMIN SEA –

Quaglino's head mixologist Federico Pasian created this elixir, wanting to give an Aviation a fresh, floral, and aromatic lift. Added complexity comes from the bergamot liqueur and juice, and the Lavender Syrup. This is a perfect cocktail to accompany oysters.

GLASSWARE: Seashell or coupette
GARNISH: Jasmine Air and samphire

- 1¼ oz. Hendrick's Gin
- ¾ oz. Italicus Rosolio di Bergamotto liqueur
- 1 teaspoon Luxardo maraschino cherry liqueur
- ⅞ oz. bergamot juice
- ½ oz. Lavender Syrup (see page 87)
- 1 dash ginger bitters
- 1 small slice fresh ginger

1. Add all of the ingredients to a cocktail shaker filled with ice and shake vigorously until chilled.

2. Double-strain into a seashell or a coupette.

3. Spoon the Jasmine Air on top of the drink and arrange the samphire on top.

JASMINE AIR: Place 9 oz. strongly brewed, cold jasmine tea and ½ teaspoon soy lecithin in a container and stir to incorporate. Strain into a large bowl and work the mixture with an immersion blender, trying to get as much air into the mixture as possible. When the mixture is very foamy, use immediately.

SCARFES BAR AT
THE ROSEWOOD
HOTEL

252 HIGH HOLBORN
HOLBORN, LONDON
WC1V 7EN

- #1 HIGH C SPRITZ -

This herbaceous cocktail was inspired by Luciano Pavarotti, the famed Italian tenor, and carries refreshing notes of bergamot and mandarin. This is an opera for your palate, and probably not a bad choice to warm up your vocal cords before taking your turn on karaoke night.

GLASSWARE: Champagne flute
GARNISH: 3 Kalamata olives

- 1 oz. Olive Leaf-Infused Hendrick's Orbium Gin
- 2 teaspoons Acqua di Cedro Nardini
- 2 teaspoons Noilly Prat Dry Vermouth
- ½ teaspoon Suze Saveur d'Autrefois
- 2 oz. Three Cents Gentlemen's Soda

1. Pour all of the ingredients into a champagne flute in the order they are listed and gently stir.

2. Garnish with the Kalamata olives.

OLIVE LEAF-INFUSED HENDRICK'S ORBIUM GIN: Place a 750 ml bottle of Hendrick's Orbium and 1 oz. of dried olive leaves in a vacuum bag and cook sous vide at 105°F for 30 minutes. Alternatively, combine 4 oz. olive leaves and the bottle of gin in a mason jar and store in a cool, dark place for 5 days. Let cool, if using the sous vide method, and strain before using or storing.

SKETCH

9 CONDUIT STREET
MAYFAIR, LONDON W1S 2XG

- BASILICO -

This refreshing herbal spritz comes courtesy of bar director Pepijn Vanden Abeele, and it's fairly low in alcohol compared to many of the powerful cocktails served in London. As you can likely guess from the name, the star here is the basil that permeates the drink.

GLASSWARE: Champagne flute
GARNISH: Basil leaf

- 4 basil leaves
- 1 oz. Tanqueray No. 10 gin
- 1 oz. Lemon Thyme-Infused Vermouth

- FeverTree Mediterranean Tonic, to top

1. Slap the basil leaves to awaken their aromatics and add them to a cocktail shaker filled with ice. Add the gin and vermouth and shake vigorously until chilled.

2. Double-strain into a champagne flute, add a few ice cubes, and top with the tonic.

3. Garnish with an additional basil leaf.

LEMON THYME-INFUSED VERMOUTH: Place 3 sprigs of lemon thyme in a 700 ml bottle of Belsazar Vermouth Dry and steep for 24 hours. Remove the sprigs of lemon thyme before using or storing.

- FIZZ KAFFIR -

A refreshing, sweet, and sour drink that was originally designed to satisfy guests who have a bit of a sweet tooth via the fruity notes. An immediate hit, it's now Purple Bar's all-time best-selling cocktail.

GLASSWARE: Highball glass
GARNISH: Dehydrated lime wheel and a maraschino cherry

- 1⅜ oz. Makrut Lime Leaf-Infused Gin
- ½ oz. pear brandy
- ½ oz. Giffard Crème de Rhubarbe
- 1 oz. cranberry juice
- ¾ oz. fresh lemon juice
- 1 egg white

1. Add all of the ingredients to a cocktail shaker filled with ice and shake vigorously until chilled.

2. Strain into the highball glass and then add ice cubes.

3. Garnish with the dehydrated lime wheel and maraschino cherry.

MAKRUT LIME LEAF-INFUSED GIN: Place 10 to 12 makrut lime leaves and a 750 ml bottle of gin in a large mason jar and stir vigorously for 1 minute. Let steep for 12 hours and strain before using or storing.

- JAPANESE WHISPERS -

Thishis is a long, refreshing, and complex cocktail that uses only Japanese spirits to provide the punchy aromas. The other ingredients combat the high-alcohol content with sweetness, citrus, and a thick texture, resulting in a concoction that is both subtle and satisfying.

GLASSWARE: Highball glass
GARNISH: Smoked paprika

- 1 ⅜ oz. shochu
- ¾ oz. Suntory Toki Whisky
- 1 oz. Passion Fruit Cordial
- 1 egg white
- ⅞ oz. Citrus Blend (equal parts fresh lime and lemon juices)

1. Add all of the ingredients to a cocktail shaker containing no ice and dry shake for 15 seconds. Add ice and shake vigorously until chilled.

2. Strain into a highball glass and add ice cubes.

3. Dust the rim of the glass with the paprika.

PASSION FRUIT CORDIAL (MAKES APPROXIMATELY 35 OZ.): Place 35 oz. Boiron Passion Fruit Puree, 7 oz. fructose, and 7 oz. caster sugar in a mason jar and stir until the fructose and sugar have dissolved.

BAR BANTER

JULIEN CASANOVA AND MARIUS POP, BARS MANAGER AND ASSISTANT BARS MANAGER SANDERSON HOTEL

When it first opened in 2000, Sanderson hotel was THE place to be. Over the years however, the cocktail boom has left it overshadowed by the many new bars in the city. It's the job of managers Julien Casanova and Marius Pop to bring back the quality of drinks and service that once made the hotel famous.

WHAT'S THE REMIT FOR YOUR JOB HERE?

JC: I joined Sanderson six months ago. It is a bit of a new challenge managing both bars, and the Sanderson is an iconic hotel in London. It's my job to help it really shine again. However, the scene is now much more competitive than it was when the hotel opened 19 years ago. There are many more places, many new bars as well as hotel bars.

MP: When Sanderson first opened, the lines were enormous. Everyone wanted to hang out at Long Bar back then as it held the title for a long time for "Longest Bar in Europe." Now we've got a new menu, new staff, and we can really do something new and unique here.

GIVE ME A QUICK SUMMARY ABOUT WHAT MAKES EACH BAR STAND OUT.

JC: Long Bar is designed so that it takes up the whole room. There are three tables at the end for people to sit [at] but that's it. The bar is the main event. Here, we aim to create simple, delicious drinks that guests can receive quickly in a great environment. Purple Bar was designed more as a traditional-yet-intimate hotel bar. It's lit by candlelight only. The interaction between the guests and staff is different here. The drinks are more sophisticated and complex.

MP: We aim to cover both ends of the spectrum with our bars. Long Bar is lively, there's lights and DJs. Purple Bar is the complete opposite, quiet and dark, with no one dancing around. Here, we can provide our guests with something colorful and personalized.

HOW DID YOU GO ABOUT DESIGNING A NEW MENU WHEN YOU ARRIVED?

JC: When I arrived, the menu here was not designed by someone in-house. They had hired an outside consultant. It was simple and very straightforward, with lots of cordials and syrups. It was meant to be served quickly. I suggested that we perhaps design something more sophisticated. Nowadays in hotels you can't just serve something with a syrup and a spirit. You need to do something with a bit more complexity.

MP: Since Julien arrived, we're looking at updating the menu and bringing things up to scratch. We're not too interested in the theatrical style of the recent past, we're looking at classic recipes, and the quality of the equipment and ice we use.

JC: Something I've seen often when menus are being designed is to lead with a concept, forcing it too much through the cocktails and the menu, and it's something inappropriate for the space. I do get it's a five-star hotel and people want something elegant to look at, something picture-friendly. We prefer to look at fresh ingredients and good infusions, without getting too over-the-top or we'll lose our guests. It's better to be able to stay flexible with what you can provide for your guests and do whatever possible to provide what suits them best.

SMITH & WHISTLE AT THE SHERATON GRAND PARK LANE HOTEL

SHERATON GRAND LONDON PARK LANE, PICCADILLY
LONDON W1J 7BX

- THE BLACK LEAF -

Motivated by bar manager Salman Ullah's childhood memories of brewing tea from the Indian subcontinent, this cocktail has a sour profile, but also depth thanks to the Earl Grey. The pear from the liqueur and the cordial adds a nice, sweet note.

GLASSWARE: Cast-iron teacup
GARNISH: Dried lavender buds

- 1⅜ oz. Copperhead Black Batch London Dry Gin
- ¾ oz. Pear & Earl Grey Cordial
- ¾ oz. fresh lemon juice
- 1 teaspoon pear liqueur
- 1 egg white

1. Add all of the ingredients to a cocktail shaker containing no ice and dry shake for 15 seconds.

2. Add ice and shake vigorously until chilled.

3. Double-strain into the teacup and garnish with dried lavender buds.

PEAR & EARL GREY CORDIAL: Place 35 oz. pear juice in a saucepan and cook over medium heat until it has reduced by half. Remove from heat and add 2 bags of Earl Grey tea and 2 cinnamon sticks. Remove the bags of tea after 5 minutes. Remove the cinnamon sticks after another 5 minutes have passed. Add an equal amount of caster sugar to the liquid and stir until it has dissolved. Strain before using or storing.

This is a sipping drink that Ullah designed with tequila lovers in mind. It's strong and citrusy while retaining a smooth, balanced flavor. A hint of chili pepper extract produces a quick kick, and nods to the animated namesake of this feisty cocktail.

GLASSWARE: 1924 miniature cocktail glass or a Pousse Café glass
GARNISH: Orange twist, orange zest, and orange oil

- 1⅜ oz. Gran Centenario Reposado Tequila
- ½ oz. Noilly Prat Dry Vermouth
- ⅜ oz. Aperol
- 1 teaspoon agave nectar
- 5 drops chili pepper extract

1. Add all of the ingredients to a mixing glass filled with ice. Using another mixing glass, utilize the Cuban roll method (see page 104) to mix the cocktail.

2. Strain over two ice cubes into the chosen glass.

3. Garnish with an orange twist, orange zest, and orange oil.

- LEMONGRASS MOJITO -

A tea house that happens to serve tea-based cocktails near Covent Garden, the Teatulia bar team created a drink that aims to recreate the fresh flavors of a Mojito with an added lemongrass kick.

GLASSWARE: Highball glass or tumbler

GARNISH: Lemongrass stalk

- 2 teaspoons loose-leaf Teatulia Organic Lemongrass Tea
- 6 fresh mint leaves
- 1¾ oz. rum (white or dark)
- ¾ oz. Simple Syrup (see page 24)
- ¾ oz. apple juice
- ¾ oz. fresh lime juice
- 1⅜ oz. seltzer water, to top

1. Place the loose-leaf tea in 1½ oz. of hot water and steep for 4 minutes.

2. Add the mint leaves to the chosen glass and muddle. Strain the tea into the glass and fill the glass halfway with ice.

3. Add the rum, syrup, apple juice, and lime juice and stir.

4. Top with the seltzer water and garnish with the lemongrass stalk.

THE WIGMORE AT THE LANGHAM HOTEL

15 LANGHAM PLACE, MARYLEBONE, LONDON W1B 3DE

– BLENDED UNION –

This offering from head bartender Stephen Georgiou was the winning drink at London Cocktail Week in 2017. The Wigmore was working with Amaro di Angostura and a coffee roaster during the week, and an elaborate iteration of this cocktail bridged those two elements with a bespoke Saison beer, a drop of honey, and mango puree. This is a more approachable version that's easy to make at home.

GLASSWARE: Beer mug

GARNISH: None

- 1⅜ oz. Amaro di Angostura
- 1⅜ oz. cold-brew coffee
- 2 teaspoons mango juice
- 2 teaspoons Honey Syrup
- 4½ oz. saison beer (Brew by Numbers 01|01 preferred, but any light-bodied saison employing new world hops will work)

1. Place all of the ingredients in a blender along with four large ice cubes and blitz until combined.

2. Pour into the beer mug.

HONEY SYRUP: Place 2 parts honey and 1 part water in a saucepan and bring to a simmer over medium heat. Cook, while stirring, until thoroughly combined. Let cool before using or storing.

ZIGGY'S AT HOTEL
CAFÉ ROYAL

68 REGENT STREET
SOHO, LONDON
W1B 4DY

– DARKNESS AND DISGRACE –

This is a fun, easy-to-make cross between a flip and an Espresso Martini, with a great, thick mouthfeel and complex taste. The combination of the Quinta do Noval Port and coffee liqueur provides a lot of rich sweetness. For the extra classy touch, cocktail architect Fabio Spinetti, the bar and beverage manager at Ziggy's, suggests tying a fresh sprig of lavender to the stem of the glass, as it will enable floral notes to hit your nose as you raise your glass to drink.

GLASSWARE: Coupette
GARNISH: Ribbon and a lavender sprig

- 1¾ oz. Diplomatico Reserva Exclusiva Rum
- ¾ oz. Quinta do Noval Port
- 2 teaspoons Bepe Tosolini Exprè Coffee Liqueur
- 2 teaspoons Simple Syrup (see page 24)
- 1 egg yolk

1. Add all of the ingredients to a cocktail shaker filled with ice and shake vigorously until chilled.

2. Strain into the coupette.

3. Use a ribbon to tie the sprig of lavender to the stem of the glass.

BAR BANTER
FABIO SPINETTI, BARS AND
BEVERAGE MANAGER, ZIGGY'S

A former bar manager at the Connaught Bar, Fabio Spinetti helped relaunch hotel Café Royal's food and beverage program. At Ziggy's, he's created a special bar in an iconic space in the history of rock.

WHERE DID THE DECISION TO GO ALL-OUT ON THE DAVID BOWIE THEME COME FROM?

David Bowie's last concert as Ziggy Stardust was in Hammersmith in 1973. He wanted to retire the character after this but no one knew it at the time. How did he announce it? He organized a party in this very room in Café Royal and everyone who was anyone was here for it, including Mick Jagger and Ringo Starr, for example. Most of the pictures that decorate the room are from that night.

The story goes that he had originally invited people for a dinner here. He was a regular. And he organized everything by word of mouth, without any invitations. At the dinner, he makes the announcement and then kicks off a party, which went on until 7 or 8 in the morning the day after—a typical story of the era.

HOW DO YOU HONOR HIS LEGACY WITH THE BAR?

After he passed away in 2016, and after a grace period following his death, we thought we'd open the bar with this idea given his history here and that he was from London, not too far from here, in Brixton. It's not so much a themed bar here, nor a shrine to his life. It's more of an homage, celebrating his legacy and his life in a space that's appropriate.

We've not changed the room much since he had his party here in the '70s. There's been a couple tweaks to the bar but not much else. All the pictures here are prints from Mick Rock, who took pictures of Bowie throughout the Ziggy era.

The names of our cocktails reflect his songs, but we didn't want to be facile and tacky by using his song titles. The cocktail names are all lyrics of his and we think each drink works well with its corresponding song. For example, our Tigers on Vaseline drink is short and sharp, which goes well with the tune the lyric is from, "Hang Onto Yourself," which is very punchy.

HOW HAS BEING BASED IN PICCADILLY CIRCUS AFFECTED BUSINESS FOR THE BAR?

It's a blessing and a curse. The footfall is massive. It doesn't get more central than this. The challenge for our other Café Royal bar, which is easy to access from the street, is that most of the people coming in are casual visitors looking for a quick drink. We're also in an unusual location, straddling Soho and Mayfair. So, in a way, you are in between two very different communities and communal identities as well. It does mean that we get the best of both, and also the worst of both.

You might get a Mayfair clientele that expects a full, well-heeled Mayfair experience, and they're not necessarily happy with a more friendly, relaxed environment; while a Soho crowd isn't necessarily looking for a five-star luxury hotel drinks experience. Our challenge is to find a balance between the two that works. We think Ziggy's does that very well.

WEST LONDON

THE CLOVER CLUB • THE MARLEYBONE
CRUSH • 47 MONKEYS • BOLIVAR SOUR •
ROYAL SIDECAR • SEASIDE MARTINI •
JOURNEY'S ESSENCE • COTTON MOUTH
KILLER • STRANGER THINGS

West London has a reputation as "posh"—unsurprising in an area with some of the world's most expensive real estate. Originally, London's wealthiest residents established themselves here to escape the smog, smoke, and general pollution that drifted toward the poorer east end of the city.

The luxury department store Harrods, London's Natural History Museum, the Royal Albert Hall, and the deer-filled Richmond Park are all located here. The Notting Hill carnival may be one of the most vibrant parties in Europe.

Aside from certain areas of West London, though (like Notting Hill), there are fewer tourists and party seekers than in other areas of the city. The bars here, then, generally have become neighborhood hangouts for local residents and/or chic destinations for Londoners on the hunt for high-quality drinks. And for those seeking the five-star treatment, there are also high-end hotels with excellent bars plying their trade here.

THE 108 BRASSERIE

108 MARYLEBONE LANE
MARYLEBONE
LONDON W1U 2QE

- THE CLOVER CLUB -

The Clover Club is a classic, pre-Prohibition cocktail named after a famous Philadelphia men's club of the era. The recipe from the bar in this Marylebone restaurant doesn't deviate much from tradition, though the clover flower adds a classy touch.

GLASSWARE: Coupe

GARNISH: Clover flower

- 1¾ oz. Tanqueray gin
- ¾ oz. fresh lemon juice
- 5 raspberries
- ¾ oz. Simple Syrup (see page 24)
- 1 egg white

1. Add all of the ingredients to a cocktail shaker and muddle the raspberries.

2. Add ice to the shaker and shake vigorously until chilled.

3. Double-strain into the coupe and garnish with the clover flower.

- THE MARYLEBONE CRUSH -

Afresh, punch-like drink that flirts with becoming a fizz. The sweetness of the cranberry juice is complemented by the cider, ginger, and mint, a combination that provides freshness, herbal undertones, and a spicy kick. A perfect drink for warmer weather.

GLASSWARE: Highball glass

GARNISH: Shaved ginger, 3 raspberries, and 4 mint leaves

- 1¾ oz. 108 Gin
- 1¼ oz. cranberry juice
- ½ oz. fresh lime juice
- Maison Sassy Cidre Brut, to top

1. Add all of the ingredients, except for the dry cider, to a cocktail shaker filled with ice and shake vigorously until chilled.

2. Strain into a highball glass filled with ice.

3. Top with the dry cider and garnish with the ginger, raspberries, and mint leaves.

**BLAKE'S BELOW AT
BLAKE'S HOTEL**

33 ROLAND GARDENS
KENSINGTON, LONDON
SW7 3PF

– 47 MONKEYS –

The 47 Monkeys is a rewarding mix of fresh and decadent, stemming from the mind of Krzysztof Cwiek. Blake's Below actually makes its lavender foam from flowers grown on the premises. There are plenty of other reasons to enjoy this one, though. Between the strawberries, basil, Champagne, and gin/sloe gin blend, this serve is a summery delight.

GLASSWARE: Wine glass
GARNISH: Lavender foam (optional),
2 sliced strawberries, and basil leaves

- 3 strawberries
- 2 to 3 basil leaves
- ⅞ oz. Monkey 47 Schwarzwald Sloe Gin
- ⅞ oz. Monkey 47 Schwarzwald Dry Gin
- ¾ oz. fresh lime juice
- 2 dashes Peychaud's Bitters
- Perrier Jouet Rosé Champagne, to top

1. Place the strawberries in a cocktail shaker and muddle them. Slap the basil leaves to awaken the aromatics and add them to the shaker along with ice, the gins, lime juice, and bitters. Shake vigorously until chilled.

2. Double-strain over ice cubes into the wine glass.

3. Top with the Champagne and, if desired, spoon the lavender foam onto the surface of the cocktail. Garnish with the sliced strawberries and basil leaves, arranging them around the glass.

- BOLIVAR SOUR -

One of GOAT Chelsea's most popular drinks, owner and bar manager Steve Manktelow replaced the rye whiskey with rum in this version of a Trinidad Sour. The nutmeg garnish helps accentuate the richness provided by the orgeat.

GLASSWARE: Coupe

GARNISH: Freshly grated nutmeg

- ⅞ oz. Mount Gay Eclipse Rum
- ⅞ oz. Angostura Bitters
- ¾ oz. Monin Almond (Orgeat) Syrup
- ⅞ oz. fresh lime juice

1. Add all of the ingredients to a cocktail shaker filled with ice and shake vigorously until chilled.

2. Strain into the coupe and grate the nutmeg over the cocktail.

LA MAISON REMY

81 FULHAM ROAD, CHELSEA
LONDON SW3 6RD

The Sidecar was invented in Paris and then introduced to London by bartender Pat McGarry, who worked at the Buck's Club after World War I. In this version of the recipe, a slightly lower amount of Cognac than usual means it should be a gentle ride.

GLASSWARE: Coupe

GARNISH: Lemon twist

- 1¼ oz. Remy Martin 1738 Cognac
- 1 oz. Cointreau
- ½ oz. fresh lemon juice

1. Add all of the ingredients in a cocktail shaker filled with ice and shake vigorously until chilled.

2. Double-strain into the coupe and garnish with the lemon twist.

– SEASIDE MARTINI –

Opso is a Greek restaurant, and Elizei Dragos and Cris Sirica designed this Martini with the Greek island of Chios in mind. In this case, the mastiha liqueur (which can only be produced on that island) adds robust herbal aromas, backed up by the softer touch of the rock samphire garnish.

GLASSWARE: Coupette

GARNISH: Rock samphire

- 3 dashes Ouzo
- 2 oz. Beefeater London Dry gin
- ½ oz. mastiha liqueur
- ¾ oz. dry vermouth

1. Pour the Ouzo into the coupette, swirl to rinse, and then chill the glass.

2. When the glass is chilled, add the remaining ingredients to a mixing glass filled with ice, stir until chilled, and strain into the coupette.

3. Garnish with the rock samphire.

POMONA'S

47 HEREFORD ROAD
LONDON W2 5AH

- JOURNEY'S ESSENCE -

J ay Decker and Tiziano Tasso start your journey with the floral Hibiscus Pisco. This is then buoyed by sweet and fruity elements, while the Muscat adds a little more body to the overall drink.

GLASSWARE: Rocks glass
GARNISH: Peach wedge

- 1½ oz. Hibiscus Pisco
- ¾ oz. Muscat
- ⅞ oz. unfiltered apple juice
- 2 teaspoons fresh lemon juice
- 2 teaspoons Simple Syrup (see page 24)
- 3 drops peach essence

1. Add all of the ingredients to a cocktail shaker filled with ice and shake vigorously until chilled.

2. Double-strain into a rocks glass containing a block of ice.

3. Garnish with the peach wedge.

HIBISCUS PISCO: Place a 750 ml bottle of pisco and ½ oz. dried hibiscus blossoms in a mason jar and let steep for 1 hour. Strain before using or storing.

TRAILER HAPPINESS

177 PORTOBELLO ROAD
NOTTING HILL
LONDON W11 2DY

- COTTON MOUTH KILLER -

Here's some tiki goodness from Tim Stones. This is one of Trailer Happiness' signature drinks, "designed to shake up your palate and clear out the cobwebs," according to bar manager Gergo Murath. The drink was also featured in the 2018 edition of the world-famous Hukilau tiki festival.

GLASSWARE: Tiki mug

GARNISH: 1¾ teaspoons Blue Wray & Nephew

- 1¾ oz. rum blend (Trailer Happiness uses a blend made of mostly lighter rums along with heavier, aged pot-still rums, aiming for a very smooth profile)
- 2 teaspoons apricot brandy
- 2 teaspoons Galliano liqueur
- 2 teaspoons Simple Syrup (see page 24)
- 1 oz. apple juice
- 1⅜ oz. guava juice

1. Add all of the ingredients to a cocktail shaker filled with ice and shake vigorously until chilled.

2. Double-strain into a tiki mug containing crushed ice.

3. Top with additional crushed ice and stir to lift the cocktail up through the ice.

4. Drizzle the Blue Wray & Nephew over the top for garnish.

BLUE WRAY & NEPHEW: Stir together 3 parts Wray & Nephew rum and 1 part blue Curaçao.

THE COURTYARD

4 FULHAM HIGH STREET
FULHAM, LONDON SW6 3LQ

Deep in West London, the quiet residential neighborhood of Fulham would not seem to be the ideal place to open an award-winning bar. Yet the four friends behind The Courtyard have managed to do just that.

Starting with an outdoor garden bar, The Courtyard team eventually expanded into the building next door. "We wanted to bring in a slice of East London vibes to the west," said founding partner Nenad Petrovic. "All around this area it's a bit quiet, a bit posh, and we thought we'd bring in something quirky and messy and see how it goes."

The outcome is an establishment that's evolved into a destination, rather than just a neighborhood hangout. The Courtyard's business is drawn primarily through online bookings and it has developed a reputation not only for its cocktails but also for its bottomless, Mexican-themed brunches. The bar's large space also features decorations based on the founders' favorite childhood movies—perfect for millennials' nostalgic sensibilities.

Then, of course, there is the superb, grand garden in the courtyard: "It started as a summer project, but we've converted it so that it also works in the winter throughout the year," says general manager Cesare Manfredini. "It's really helped create a fun environment."

Adding to its luster, the bar has won multiple awards from notable online guides *Time Out* and London's *DesignMyNight*, honors that have driven further success, according to Manfredini: "The moment we got the award for 'Best Outdoor Space' in London with *Time Out* our bookings exploded. From one day to another we went from 100 bookings to 500. So business is booming now."

- STRANGER THINGS -

This sweet crowd-pleaser was engineered by Cesare Manfredini and Fabio Fioravanti. The fruitiness supplied by the strawberry-laced vodka and passion fruit puree makes the nice, dry finish provided by the Prosecco essential to the drink.

GLASSWARE: Lightbulb glass or champagne flute

GARNISH: Raspberry

- 1⅜ oz. Strawberry Tea-Infused Vodka
- 1⅜ oz. passion fruit puree
- ¾ oz. Simple Syrup (see page 24)
- Prosecco, to top

1. Add the vodka, passion fruit puree, and syrup to a cocktail shaker filled with ice and shake vigorously until chilled.

2. Double-strain into a lightbulb glass or champagne flute.

3. Top with the Prosecco and garnish with a raspberry that has been speared by a cocktail straw.

STRAWBERRY TEA-INFUSED VODKA: Place 3 bags of strawberry tea in a 750 ml bottle of Reyka Vodka. Shake and let steep for 24 hours. Remove the tea bags before using or storing.

NORTH LONDON

CAOL ILA COSMO • ENRIQUE THE V •
THE COOLCUMBER • GRASSHOPPER NO.
245 • RUM BA BA • ELECTRIC EARL •
LONDON HAZE • PEACH TEA • TRINIDAD
SWIZZLE • EARL OF SEVILLE • PIN-UP
ZOMBIE • THE VERY HUNGRY
MANZANILLA

North London is to an extent London's most "recent" region, with development driven by the establishment of railway networks in the mid-19th century. These days, it sometimes is dismissed as "bougie" by Londoners elsewhere. Like much of the city, North London has transformed rapidly over recent decades (especially the area around King's Cross Station), and it's a great place to visit.

Camden hosts a world-renowned market in addition to phenomenal music venues and bars. The British Library is a true architectural gem, and the neighborhood bristles with superb, world-famous museums. There's even Platform 9¾ in the King's Cross Station for Harry Potter fans.

The bars here also offer a wide variety of approaches to creating great cocktails. Some examples: At Little Mercies, advanced preparation with specialized equipment means an easy, fast pour of complex drinks. BYOC Camden lets you bring your own spirits that the bartenders then incorporate into bespoke cocktails, while Laki Kane offers a modern, London take on tiki.

In short, there's something here for everyone to enjoy.

BLACK ROCK

9 CHRISTOPHER STREET, FINSBURY
LONDON EC2A 2BS

- CAOL ILA COSMO -

On the surface, this creation from the Black Rock team may resemble the drink popularized on *Sex and the City*, but once you throw smoky single malt in for the vodka, it's a whole new ballgame.

GLASSWARE: Nick & Nora glass
GARNISH: None

- 1⅛ oz. Caol Ila 12-Year-Old Single Malt Scotch Whisky
- ½ oz. Cointreau
- ⅝ oz. cranberry juice
- ⅝ oz. 20:1 citric acid solution (by weight, water:citric acid)

1. Chill a Nick & Nora glass before pouring the cocktail ingredients into the glass and stirring them together.

BAR BANTER
THOM SOLBERG, BAR MANAGER
BLACK ROCK

Black Rock is one of London's premier whisky bars, with patrons picking their drams from cabinets filled with beautiful bottles organized by flavor profile. Thom Solberg manages both the impressive whisky selection and the excellent whisky cocktails served downstairs and in the ground-floor "tavern."

WHAT COCKTAILS DO YOU OFFER IN A WHISKY BAR?

We're a whisky bar, so all our cocktails are about the whisky. In the basement, we serve six cocktails and six highball variations. Our cocktails are a shorter style of drink, while the highballs are longer, refreshing serves. We don't bother with cute names or puns or anything like that. We name them after the flavor profile of the drink. The cocktails are a great way to also get into whisky if it's something that doesn't normally interest you.

In the tavern upstairs, the cocktails have names, but also are whisky cocktails. They are twists on the classics, all easy serves that taste delicious. For example, we're quite proud of our West Vesper, a Martini that's made without gin or vodka. Using whisky products, we've managed to make something very Vesper-esque.

We've also eliminated garnishes from the drinks, though we do have some oils that we spray on things. But we've taken away a lot of the stuff that we don't think is needed so we can cut down on unnecessary waste.

There are way more ways to introduce orange aromas than just using fresh orange juice, which really needs a lot of oranges. Another example: When we use aquafaba (the liquid that results when beans are cooked in water, usually referring to chickpeas) to thicken the drink, we use the chickpeas as well to make hummus that we can serve customers, too.

YOU HAVE A DIFFERENT WAY OF ORGANIZING YOUR WHISKY SELECTION THAN MOST BARS, RIGHT?

We categorize whisky by flavor profiles rather than by other methods like the region. So, categories like "smoke," or "fruity." We don't have a menu. This helps change the language on how we talk about the drink, but also gives someone who doesn't necessarily know much about whisky a way to approach it effectively. To lead with flavor makes more sense.

In the Black Rock Tavern, however, we've got 54 whiskies here, all pretty affordable, while downstairs has 400 bottles with cabinets that people can explore. The enormous tree-trunk table in the middle is pretty cool, too.

We're going for good, old-school hospitality with a whisky angle. We're mixing that with whisky because we see whisky as something that a lot of people have a strong interest in and a lot of people care a great deal about. We want to present it in a way that's simpler and easier. It doesn't require any prerequisite knowledge. We're always happy to have whisky beginners come through and help them with their journey, suggest things that they might enjoy, and encourage active exploration of the category. It's great fun because we love whisky as much as anyone who comes down to visit us.

BOBBY FITZPATRICK

273 WEST END LANE
WEST HAMPSTEAD
LONDON NW6 1QS

– ENRIQUE THE V –

The cocktails at Bobby Fitzpatrick are named after members of Bobby's (fictional) family. According to cocktail creator Alessandro Paludet, Enrique is the fifth husband of Bobby's mother, Cynthia, and is also the 45-year-old gardener in the Florida apartment complex where they live. For those wondering, Cynthia's in her late 80s.

GLASSWARE: Large coupe
GARNISH: Slice of dehydrated pineapple and absinthe mist

- 1 oz. Del Maguey Vida Mezcal
- ¾ oz. Aperol
- ⅞ oz. fresh lime juice
- ½ oz. Rich Simple Syrup (see page 24, use demerara sugar)
- 1¼ oz. pineapple juice
- 3 dashes absinthe
- 1 egg white

1. Add all of the ingredients to a cocktail shaker containing no ice and dry shake for 15 seconds.

2. Add ice and shake vigorously until chilled.

3. Double-strain into the large coupe.

4. Garnish with the slice of dehydrated pineapple and a spritz of absinthe.

BYOC CAMDEN

11-13 CAMDEN HIGH STREET, KING'S CROSS
LONDON NW1 7JE

- THE COOLCUMBER -

Wat makes BYOC Camden, owned by Steeven Danilo Rosales and Alexander Trygubenko, stand out is that it lets you bring your own booze, which the bar will use to make a bespoke cocktail. However, when pressed for a recipe, bar manager Marvin Morgan offered up this refreshingly fruity creation, which gets a little more depth from the cardamom bitters.

GLASSWARE: Rocks glass
GARNISH: Basil leaves and (optional) lime wedge

- 2⅛ oz. Bobby's Schiedam Dry Gin (or any London Dry gin)
- ¾ oz. fresh lime juice
- ½ oz. cucumber juice
- 1¼ oz. lychee juice
- ½ oz. Bottlegreen Elderflower Cordial
- 3 dashes cardamom bitters

1. Add all of the ingredients to a cocktail shaker filled with ice and shake vigorously until chilled.

2. Strain over ice into a rocks glass.

3. Garnish with basil leaves and, if desired, a lime wedge.

CROQUE MONSIEUR AT LOST BOYS PIZZA

245 EVERSHOLT STREET
LONDON NW1 1BA

Some food and drink pairings are perfect and make absolute sense. Wine and cheese or whisky and chocolate, for example. Then, of course, there is absinthe and pizza.

Croque Monsieur is an absinthe bar inside a 1980s, vampire-themed pizzeria, Lost Boys Pizza. Somehow, it works—probably because it's in Camden. Liverpool-born co-founder Pete Crozier-Clucas (aka "Chief Vampire") had always dreamed of opening an absinthe bar. But instead, he and co-founder Alex Fisher invested their time and energy into Lost Boys Pizza. When the offer came to open a new location with an additional basement space, the opportunity was irresistible: "We were shown a 'storeroom' in the basement which had a separate entrance from the street and a stained-glass window," Crozier-Clucas says. "We knew immediately this space would be Croque Monsieur."

This small, 16-cover bar not only serves excellent absinthe cocktails, but also regularly hosts themed nights and parties, including movie nights, hip-hop karaoke, and Dungeons & Dragons sessions. There are also many hats hung on the bar's walls and people are encouraged to wear them. "Camden has a Gothic vibe and it embraces the absinthe culture readily," says Crozier-Clucas.

Led by bar manager Jenny Griffiths (aka "Chief Fairy," pictured), Croque Monsieur reworks old classics, which are often given an absinthe-related twist. There is a respectable absinthe menu as well if you feel like drinking alcohol over 65% ABV. No wonder this pizza joint is a little zany.

- GRASSHOPPER NO. 245 -

Jenny Griffiths dreamed up this extremely strong Grasshopper, which is so robust the creamy texture may be all it has in common with its ancestor. Nonetheless, the aromatic, herbal absinthe and Green Chartreuse are enhanced with hints of chocolate for a truly decadent serve.

GLASSWARE: Highball glass
GARNISH: Cinnamon stick

- ¾ oz. Pernod Absinthe
- ¾ oz. Green Chartreuse
- ½ oz. La Maison Fontaine Chocolat
- 2 dashes chocolate bitters
- 3 dashes Ms. Better's Bitters Miraculous Foamer
- 1¾ oz. soy milk

1. Add all of the ingredients to a cocktail shaker filled with ice and shake vigorously until chilled.

2. Strain into a highball glass filled with ice.

3. Garnish with the cinnamon stick.

DRINK, SHOP & DO

9 CALEDONIAN ROAD
ISLINGTON, LONDON N1 9DX

It's tricky to describe Drink, Shop & Do. Part café, part activity studio, part craft boutique, and part cocktail bar. Does that make it clear?

Founded in 2010 and located in King's Cross, it has been a big success with Londoners of all stripes, including A-list celebrities. Among this latter set, Rowan Atkinson of *Blackadder* and *Mr. Bean* fame hosted a secret, 50-person gig at the bar, and supermodel Cara Delevingne once held a Christmas party here.

Director and founder Coralie Sleap credits the unusual blend of food, drinks, and activities that occurs in this quirky space for its longevity, even as King's Cross has undergone massive redevelopment in the time they have been in the neighborhood. "We were here before any of the new development in King's Cross had begun," Sleap says. "When we arrived, it was a gritty place and I think that added to the appeal of bringing your friends to a beautiful, slightly hidden bar in contrast to the surroundings."

The bar was born when Sleap decided to start boozy, midweek activity nights together with "bored and broke friends," collectively known as Art Club. When she got the opportunity to bring the fun of Art Club into a pop-up venue, she took it and hasn't looked back since.

When you visit, be sure to try the cocktails, which cover a variety of styles and flavors, and don't miss out on the legendary cakes, too. Nice combination.

amed after the French cake, this cocktail created by Ben Ghosn is not as sickly sweet as you'd think considering the ingredients. The sharpness of the rum and all the creamy elements make it a perfect fit for pairing with the cakes made famous by Drink, Shop & Do. Think of this as part of an adult version of milk and cookies.

GLASSWARE: Rocks glass

GARNISH: Passion fruit slice and a mint sprig

- 1½ oz. Appleton Estate rum
- 1½ oz. heavy cream
- 1 oz. Monin Almond Syrup (Orgeat)
- ½ oz. fresh lemon juice
- 1¼ oz. passion fruit puree
- 2 dashes Peychaud's Bitters

1. Add all of the ingredients to a cocktail shaker filled with ice and shake vigorously until chilled.

2. Double-strain into a rocks glass filled with ice.

3. Garnish with a passion fruit slice and a sprig of mint.

- ELECTRIC EARL -

This psychedelic cocktail creates a balance between bitter flavors, from the Lady Grey-infused liqueur and grapefruit juice, and herbal freshness. Try to find and use the electric daisy, too—it actually zaps your tongue. "I have to admit it's quite a strange, spicy sensation. But a nice kind of strange, though," says founder Marian Beke, architect of the Electric Earl.

GLASSWARE: Lightbulb glass or a snifter
GARNISH: Purple shiso leaf, LED ice cubes, and dried electric daisy

- 1¾ oz. Sansho-Infused Oxley Gin
- ½ oz. fresh lime juice
- ⅞ oz. fresh pink grapefruit juice
- 3 dashes Electric Bitters
- 2 teaspoons Lady Grey-Infused Fortunela
- 1½ oz. Gibson Grass Cordial
- 1 splash shiso vinegar

1. Add all of the ingredients to a mixing glass filled with ice and, using another mixing glass, utilize the Cuban roll method to mix the cocktail (see page 104).

2. Pour the cocktail into the chosen glassware.

3. Garnish with a purple shiso leaf, LED ice cubes, and an electric daisy.

SANSHO-INFUSED OXLEY GIN: Add ½ oz. of chopped sansho pepper to a 750 ml bottle of Oxley Gin and let steep for 3 to 5 days. Strain before using or storing.

THE GIBSON

44 OLD STREET
LONDON EC1V 9AQ

LADY GREY-INFUSED FORTUNELA: Add 6 oz. loose-leaf Lady Grey tea into a 500 ml bottle of Fortunella Golden Orange Liqueur and let steep for 30 to 45 minutes. Strain before using or storing.

GIBSON GRASS CORDIAL: Place 25 oz. tonic water in a saucepan and bring to a boil. Add 1 small handful of each of the following: kukicha tea, prunella leaves, shiso leaves, eucalyptus leaves, chopped lemongrass, makrut lime leaves, lemon balm leaves, and lemon thyme leaves, reduce heat, and simmer for 15 minutes. Strain and add 26½ oz. sugar to the mixture. Stir until the sugar has dissolved and let cool completely before using or storing. The cordial will keep in the refrigerator for up to 1 month.

KEYSTONE CRESCENT

28 KEYSTONE CRESCENT
ISLINGTON, LONDON N1 9DT

– LONDON HAZE –

Dimitris Gryparis's inspiration for The London Haze was The Great Smog of 1952, when air pollution shut London down for four days in December and caused significant health issues. Gryparis wanted to counter the depressing effects of London pollution and leave the customer feeling uplifted and cosseted.

GLASSWARE: Tumbler

GARNISH: Lit joint (optional)

- ⅞ oz. Pineapple-Infused Sailor Jerry
- ⅞ oz. Caña Brava 3-Year-Old Rum
- ⅞ oz. passion fruit puree
- ¾ oz. fresh lime juice
- ¾ oz. Vanilla Syrup

1. Add all of the ingredients to a cocktail shaker filled with ice and shake vigorously until chilled.

2. Double-strain into a tumbler filled with ice. Garnish with a lit joint. Unless, of course, it's illegal.

PINEAPPLE-INFUSED SAILOR JERRY: Place a 750 ml bottle of Sailor Jerry and 10½ oz. chopped pineapple in a vacuum bag, vacuum seal it, and let it sit for 3 days. Or place the rum and pineapple in a mason jar, seal, and let sit for 1 week. Strain before using or storing.

VANILLA SYRUP: Add 2 tablespoons pure vanilla extract to 2 cups of Simple Syrup (see page 24) after the sugar has dissolved. Let the syrup cool completely before using or storing

LITTLE MERCIES

20 BROADWAY PARADE
CROUCH END, LONDON N8 9DE

Little Mercies owner Alan Sherwood credits Three Sheets proprietors Max and Noel Venning, as well as Scout co-founder Matt Whiley, as his main inspirations when he opened Little Mercies.

His career did not begin with bartending: "Business-wise, the bar is the second company I have owned and founded," Sherwood said. "Before moving into hospitality, I owned a design studio focusing on digital and e-commerce design. I ran that for eight years before deciding I needed a change."

Little Mercies, with an understated, minimalist atmosphere reminiscent of the Vennings' acclaimed Three Sheets (see page 309), has drawn rave reviews for cocktails that seem simple to make at the bar, but actually require extensive advance preparation, including complex infusions and fat-washes. As a result, the drinks seem like fun serves that can be enjoyed every day, rather than the special, one-time experiences that they are.

Despite the plaudits for his drinks, Sherwood is justifiably proud of another element of the bar: "The thing I am most proud of at the bar is our food menu. Most people don't realize that we are a fully functioning kitchen with food till 11 pm. We have two chefs putting out some of the best plates of food I've had. And yeah, I might be biased, but I think it's true!"

- PEACH TEA -

A perfect summertime thirst-quencher, owner Alan Sherwood's innovation is also the go-to drink for the Little Mercies bar team. This recipe is for a single serving, but the bar makes this as a batch drink because of the preparation involved. Feel free to follow their lead and whip up a large amount of the Peach Cordial.

GLASSWARE: Highball glass
GARNISH: Lemon wedge

- ½ oz. Silver Needle-Infused Ocho Blanco
- ½ oz. Ocho Blanco Tequila
- ¾ oz. Peach Cordial
- 1 drop clary sage tincture
- 1 dash Merlet Crème de Pêche
- Club soda, to top

1. Pour all of the ingredients, except for the club soda, into a highball glass filled with ice and stir.

2. Top with the club soda and garnish with the lemon wedge.

SILVER NEEDLE-INFUSED OCHO BLANCO: Place 10½ oz. Ocho Blanco Tequila and ⅛ oz. loose-leaf silver needle tea in a mason jar and let steep for 24 hours. Strain before using or storing.

PEACH CORDIAL (ADJUST AMOUNTS AS NEEDED): Pit 4½ lbs. of peaches and puree them. Stir 2 teaspoons of Pectinex Ultra SP-L into the puree and then spin the mixture in a centrifuge at 4200 rpm for 20 minutes. Strain the resulting juice through a coffee filter. Add 53 oz. caster sugar and 1 oz. citric acid to the clarified juice and stir until the sugar has dissolved. Stir in 10 drops of galbanum tincture and use or store.

RACKETEER

105 KING'S CROSS ROAD
LONDON WC1X 9LR

- TRINIDAD SWIZZLE -

This is an exotic, fruity take on a Bermuda Rum Swizzle from Marco Torre, easy drinking and really refreshing. The sweetness is balanced by the acidity of the lime and passion fruit.

GLASSWARE: Highball glass

GARNISH: Orange slice, cherry, and a mint sprig

- ⅞ oz. white rum
- ¾ oz. dark rum
- 2 teaspoons crème de pêche
- ½ oz. fresh lime juice
- 2 teaspoons Raspberry & Pomegranate Shrub
- ½ oz. passion fruit seeds

1. Add all of the ingredients to a highball glass filled with crushed ice and stir.

2. Garnish with an orange slice, a cherry, and a sprig of mint.

RASPBERRY & POMEGRANATE SHRUB: Place 10½ oz. pomegranate juice, 10 oz. caster sugar, and 1½ oz. raspberry vinegar in a saucepan and warm over medium heat, stirring until the sugar has dissolved. Remove from heat and let cool to room temperature before using or storing.

- EARL OF SEVILLE -

Anna Gaglione's elegant cocktail was selected for the semifinal of the Chivas Masters UK 2019 competition. That endorsement is due to its multiple layers, with an emphasis on subtle citrus touches.

GLASSWARE: Nick & Nora glass
GARNISH: Dehydrated apple slice

- 1¾ oz. Earl Grey-Infused Chivas Regal
- ⅞ oz. fresh lemon juice
- 1 teaspoon Italicus Rosolio di Bergamotto liqueur
- 1 teaspoon Rich Simple Syrup (see page 24)
- ½ teaspoon Fernet-Branca
- 1 tablespoon bitter orange marmalade
- Apple Foam, to top

1. Chill a Nick & Nora glass.

2. Add all of the ingredients, except for the Apple Foam, to a cocktail shaker and shake vigorously until chilled.

3. Double-strain into the chilled glass and top with the Apple Foam.

4. Garnish with the dehydrated apple slice.

EARL GREY-INFUSED CHIVAS REGAL: Place 1¾ cups Chivas Regal 12 and 3 bags of Earl Grey tea (or ⅛ oz. loose-leaf) in a mason jar and let steep for 30 minutes. Strain before using or storing.

APPLE FOAM: Place 14 oz. apple juice, ⅛ oz. egg white powder, and 2 teaspoons Rich Simple Syrup in a whipping siphon and use 1 charge to whip until foamy.

LAKI KANE

144-145 UPPER STREET, ISLINGTON, LONDON N1 1QY

Given Londoners' stereotypically hectic lifestyles, a tiki bar in a city known for its intensity seems both oxymoronic and entirely appropriate. Laki Kane's goal is to give you five-star tropical resort treatment through the power of their drinks, which may well be what most bustling Londoners need.

The bar is the brainchild of Bulgarian co-founder Georgi Radev, who opened Laki Kane with Sam Robson and Steve Kyprianou. He takes the concept of tiki seriously, so much so it causes some tongue-in-cheek immodesty: "Tiki is a genius idea that is still absolutely relevant. I have traveled all over the world teaching people about rum, tropical drinks, and modern tiki. I've been to many tropical locations, and I wanted to recreate tropical destinations in Laki Kane while introducing a modern vision for the tiki lifestyle."

Radev's vision has expressed itself in a two-floor tropical paradise mixing global influences from around world—from Polynesia to Jamaica. There are rope ladders, bongo drum tables, and seemingly endless rivers of incredible rum. It even boasts an on-site micro-distillery where people can take part in rum master classes.

As for the cocktails, Radev's interpretation of tiki combines tropical influences and modern technology: "We are using ingredients like soursop, cupuassu, jackfruit, sapodilla, sorrel, cacao fruit, and mauby bark to take you on a tropical journey of true flavors. We also don't use refined sugar in our cocktails. We mill our own sugarcane juice and use natural, unrefined sugars including honey, agave, date syrup, and monk fruit. We're even making our own syrups in our laboratory using these natural sweeteners and unique tropical fruits."

The outcome is an approach to tiki drinks that adds a unique tropical twist to London's exploding bar scene.

- PIN-UP ZOMBIE -

Inspired by the Zombie, the tiki classic invented by Don the Beachcomber in 1934, this is meant to be a more gentle version that still hits hard. Co-founder Georgi Radev made a conscious choice to create a tiki drink that doesn't use typical tiki ingredients, hoping to propel the genre into a new era.

GLASSWARE: Pin-up Zombie mug or a tiki mug
GARNISH: ½ passion fruit husk, 3 pineapple leaves, passion fruit, coconut sugar, rum, absinthe, and a dusting of cinnamon

- ⅞ oz. Bacardi Añejo Cuatro rum
- ⅞ oz. Pusser's Gunpowder Proof rum
- 2 teaspoons Santa Teresa 1796 rum
- ½ oz. Quaglia Liquore di Ciliegia cherry liqueur
- 2 teaspoons Quaglia Liquore Pino Mugo pine liqueur
- 2 teaspoons Falernum
- 1 oz. Monin Passion Fruit Syrup
- ¾ oz. fresh pink grapefruit juice
- ½ oz. fresh lime juice

1. Place all of the ingredients in a cocktail shaker filled with ice and shake vigorously until chilled.

2. Strain over crushed ice into the chosen glassware.

3. Add more crushed ice and place the passion fruit husk and pineapple leaves on top.

4. Add a spoonful of passion fruit and a generous pinch of coconut sugar.

5. Mix together 2 teaspoons each of rum and absinthe, pour the mixture into the husk, and light it with a long match. Sprinkle cinnamon over the flames.

- THE VERY HUNGRY -
MANZANILLA

Paraphrased from the famed children's book by Eric Carle, *The Very Hungry Caterpillar*, this very grown-up drink has plenty of depth, belying the green coloring. Also, these might be the best garnishes in the book.

GLASSWARE: Highball glass
GARNISH: Perforated mint sprig and a candy caterpillar

- 1¼ oz. Plantation 3 Stars white rum
- ½ oz. Manzanilla Amontillado Sherry
- ¾ oz. fresh lime juice
- ½ oz. Sage & Mint Agave
- Seltzer water, to top

1. Add all of the ingredients, except for the seltzer water, to a cocktail shaker filled with ice and shake vigorously until chilled.

2. Double-strain into a highball glass and fill the glass with ice.

3. Top with the seltzer water and garnish with the perforated sprig of mint and the candy caterpillar.

SAGE & MINT AGAVE (ADJUST AMOUNTS AS NEEDED):
Place 9 oz. agave, 2½ oz. water, 50 mint leaves, and 8 sage leaves in a blender and puree until smooth. Strain through a piece of cheesecloth before using or storing.

BAR BANTER
STUART BINKS
HEAD BARTENDER AND
CO-FOUNDER, VICTORY MANSION

One of four friends who started Victory Mansion, Stuart Binks and his co-founders have invested their blood, sweat, and tears to create a little neighborhood bar that has become known for its excellent, literature-themed drinks and tapas-style food. The bar name comes from George Orwell's *Nineteen Eighty-Four*, the moniker for the dilapidated residence of the main character, Winston Smith.

HOW DID YOU END UP HERE?

I started bartending 19 years ago when I was at university. It was a good job to have while studying. It was also a great job with which to travel the world. I went and lived in New York, then I lived in Vancouver. I moved here 10 years ago with my partner at the time and I've stuck around since.

In my time working here, I've found that the bar scene in London is leading the way globally. London has some of the best bars in the world. So, four years ago a group of us got together and decided that we wanted to open our own place. We all chipped in what little money we had and we did all of the renovations ourselves and managed to open our own bar.

HOW HAS IT BEEN OVER THOSE FOUR YEARS?

We're just a small neighborhood bar which, in my opinion, offers good drinks and good food. Being located where we are, it's a little bit too far north of Dalston and a little bit too far south of Church Street [a busy street in Stoke Newington] for it to be more of a destination. It's low-key, and locals keep the place going. There isn't a day that I don't know at least half the people who come through the door. I personally know lots of our customers.

CAN YOU TELL ME A LITTLE BIT ABOUT YOUR COCKTAIL MENU, HOW IT HAS DEVELOPED OVER TIME, AND WHAT YOU GUYS THINK ABOUT WHEN DEVELOPING THE MENU?
Generally, we take the classics and put a twist on them, as these drinks are classics for a reason. We're just playing with the flavors, contrasting or complementing profiles. We wiggle in bits and pieces that we think might work and try it, taste it. If it doesn't work, we try, try again until it works.

We aim to get a broad spectrum of flavors when we write a menu, too. If you create a menu that only caters to what you like, you miss a broad range of new customers. We used to make a drink that I thought was absolutely disgusting but we had one person who came back again and again for that drink and got really upset when we changed the menu and shifted out the drink.

Taste is such a personal thing. It's completely subjective. So, we start from scratch with every menu and try to hit every point of the spectrum. Maybe something that's slightly sweeter than I would like and something on the more bitter end and we come up with a result that can please everybody.

SOUTH LONDON

THE MARATHON MAN • KOOL HERC •

BUMBLE BEER SOUR • LET'S GET

LAMBIC LIT • BAIJIU • CAPTAIN

AWESOME • GINGER BEER & BASIL

MOJITO • BUTTERED RUM • JIRO

DREAMS OF SUSHI • ZIGGY STARDUST

The history and development of South London begins in Southwark, on the southern end of the London Bridge, which eventually developed outward and connected with other villages south of the city. It was also a foul-smelling section until well into the 20th century, home to multiple heavy industries and feared institutions—tanneries, timber yards, prisons, and asylums among them.

Those sites have been fully redeveloped, with new investment divorcing many of South London's neighborhoods from an infamous past as recent as 20 years ago.

Regarding drinks, South London is booming. It is marked by new breweries and distilleries and plenty of bars serving their products. While you will find excellent luxury bars around London Bridge and South Bank, most of South London's best cocktail spots are small, independent, and largely unheralded neighborhood bars serving cheap drinks (by London standards) of the highest quality.

BATCH

56 PECKHAM RYE
PECKHAM, LONDON SE15 4JR

On entering this Peckham bar, you will be struck by a singular impression: it manages to look both charming and shabby at the same time. General manager Phil Sanders explains that they are planning a gradual but complete renovation of the bar, as Batch was originally meant to be a temporary project: "We ran it like a Christmas pop-up, with an original plan to just come in for a few months. But as we kept investing more money, we kept extending the lease. And we kept making seasonal changes to the space, too."

Two years later, Batch is here to stay—and that's a good thing: "Now we're thinking of applying for a seven-year tenancy," said Sanders. "But it means reworking the infrastructure we have in place, which still is built a little like a pop-up."

Batch, as can be guessed by the name, mainly serves cocktails that have been pre-prepared in batches—though they can still whip up a Negroni if you want them to. The bar also carries small-but-superb (and very affordable by London standards) whisky and gin lists.

Over time, Batch has outgrown its pop-up roots and matured into a neighborhood bar that connects with the Peckham community, which has become Sanders's favorite aspect of his job: "Every single day, good people walk through that door. That's the best thing about this place. The community in Peckham here is fantastic."

A perfect dessert cocktail, Batch bar manager Phil Sanders created the Marathon Man to celebrate the 10th anniversary of London Cocktail Week. It's an indulgent, Snickers-flavored birthday cake in a glass, and extremely filling.

GLASSWARE: Rocks glass
GARNISH: Half a miniature Snickers bar

- 1 oz. FEW Bourbon
- ¾ oz. Kahlùa
- 2 teaspoons Monin Almond Syrup (Orgeat)
- ¾ oz. Frangelico
- ¾ oz. Mozart Dark Chocolate liqueur
- 1 tablespoon peanut butter
- 1½ oz. milk
- 1 miniature Snickers bar

1. Add all of the ingredients to a blender along with two quality ice cubes and pulverize until there are fine bubbles throughout and all the ice has been thoroughly incorporated.

2. Pour over ice into a rocks glass.

3. Garnish with half of a miniature Snickers bar.

FUNKIDORY

42 PECKHAM RYE, PECKHAM
LONDON SE15 4JR

– KOOL HERC –

This is a spin on a White Russian created by Funkidory co-founder Sergio Leanza, reflecting the rich Caribbean heritage in the neighborhood of Peckham. It's named after Jamaican-born DJ Clive Campbell aka DJ Kool Herc, who famously pioneered what's known as the breakbeat—a technique of isolating, looping, and juggling the percussion-led sections of a record, an innovation that inspired a new dance style in the '70s. If you can't find the Supermalt called for in this cocktail, use another malted drink to make the reduction.

GLASSWARE: Rocks glass
GARNISH: Ground mace

- 1½ oz. Jamaican pot-still gold rum
- 1 teaspoon Jamaican overproof white rum
- 1 oz. Plantain-Infused Supermalt Reduction
- Coconut Cream Blend, to top

1. Add the rum and Supermalt reduction to a rocks glass.

2. Fill the glass with ice and top with the Coconut Cream Blend.

3. Generously sprinkle the ground mace on top for garnish.

PLANTAIN-INFUSED SUPERMALT REDUCTION: Use 1 chopped plantain for every 9 oz. of reduced Supermalt. Place the desired amount of Supermalt in a saucepan and reduce by two-thirds over medium heat. Remove from heat and add the chopped plantain. Let steep for 3 hours and strain before using or storing.

COCONUT CREAM BLEND: Mix equal parts coconut cream and double cream in a small bowl (enough to top the glass or more if making a large batch or multiple cocktails). Stir in 3 dashes of Tonka bean extract and use immediately.

BAR BANTER
SERGIO LEANZA
CO-FOUNDER, FUNKIDORY

Funkidory co-founders Sergio and his wife, Anna, are the only full-time employees at their bar, which they established from scratch. Within its short history, it has already become renowned for its great drinks and music, and Funkidory is slowly gathering an increasing number of award nominations as more people discover and rave about this special little bar.

HOW DID YOU DECIDE TO OPEN A BAR TOGETHER?
Anna and I met right before she got a job for an events company. She didn't have a bar background. I left my cocktail bar job and I worked for the same company on a freelance basis. So, from that time we realized that we could actually work together and we've managed to live together for six years without killing each other. We also wanted to stop working for other people and do our own thing.

We were very lucky when we were looking for a venue. When this place came up, cheaper than the usual prices, it was perfect because it was also between some restaurants that we love.

We wanted to make a place where we could play the music that we like, use the colors we like and the art that we like without anyone telling us what to do. It's been tough in that we had no investors, relying on the help of family and friends. But it's been amazing so far.

CAN YOU TELL ME ABOUT YOUR COCKTAIL MENU AND HOW YOU DEVELOPED IT?
We try to bring the multicultural history and music of Peckham to life with our cocktails.

One of our signature drinks, the Kalakuta Sour, is inspired by the great Nigerian musician Fela Kuti. I love him! I discovered him through the work of Cream and Ginger Baker, and then I became obsessed with Africa as a whole. I went to all the local African shops here to learn more about the music and also about the ingredients. A lot of the ladies who run the shops thought I was a bit crazy.

With the Kalakuta Sour I'm using bitter leaf as a tincture spray to create a strong, bitter, and grassy flavor in a whisky sour–style cocktail. I'm aiming to take flavors found in Nigerian beverages and translate that to the drink.

Another example is our Golden Mile cocktail—it used to be called Rye Lane here in Peckham—and it uses some local market ingredients. It's a twist on a cocktail called Gold Rush that was created at Milk & Honey in New York.

SO YOUR CLIENTELE IS MOSTLY PECKHAM LOCALS?

Yes. Fortunately, we're in an area with a lot of footfall. We get a lot of people who wander in by accident, or come in and say "I live around the corner and had no idea that you were here!"

We're just focusing on what we do. At one point we actually found out we were number 48 on a list for "London's 50 Best Bars," and we had no idea for months.

It's just me and Anna running everything, though sometimes we'll bring in a third person on Fridays and Saturdays. So it gives me the time to be able to send more drinks out, while still being able to chat with people and make sure that they have a good time with us.

- BUMBLE BEER SOUR -

Co-founder Steve Wheeler intended this drink to serve as a winter cocktail that would showcase all of gin's potential flavor profiles: citrus, floral, spicy, and sweet.

GLASSWARE: Coupette

GARNISH: Bee pollen and a lavender sprig

- 1½ oz. gin (G & B uses Tarquin's Cornish Dry)
- ¾ oz. fresh lemon juice
- ⅞ oz. Honey Beer Syrup
- ½ oz. Drambuie
- 1 dash chili oil
- 2 drops orange blossom honey
- 1 egg white

1. Add all of the ingredients to a cocktail shaker containing no ice and dry shake for 15 seconds. Add ice and shake vigorously until chilled.

2. Double-strain into the coupette.

3. Garnish with bee pollen and a sprig of lavender.

HONEY BEER SYRUP: Place 3 parts honey beer (Honey Brown is the most popular example of a honey beer), 2 parts sugar, and 1 part honey in a saucepan and bring to a simmer, stirring until the sugar has dissolved. Remove from heat and let cool before using or storing.

nother offering from Wheeler, this one created to showcase beer's potential as a legitimate cocktail ingredient. The sour beer not only lengthens the cocktail, it adds spritz and sourness for balance and a cider-like fruitiness. It's named after the G & B staff's fondness for staying late on a Sunday night and drinking Belgian sour beers.

GLASSWARE: Julep cup
GARNISH: Dehydrated lime wheel and a mint sprig

- 1⅜ oz. blackberry gin
- 1 oz. Baked Apple Chai Syrup
- ½ oz. fresh lime juice

- Sour beer, to top (G & B uses Petrus Aged Pale)

1. Add all of the ingredients, except for the beer, to a cocktail shaker filled with ice and shake vigorously until chilled.

2. Strain into a julep cup filled to the top with crushed ice.

3. Top with the sour beer.

4. Garnish with the dehydrated lime wheel and sprig of mint.

BAKED APPLE CHAI SYRUP: Brew chai tea and add 1 dehydrated apple slice for every 3½ oz. of tea. Add 2 parts sugar for every 1 part of tea and stir until the sugar has dissolved. Strain before using or storing.

BAR BANTER
STEVE WHEELER
OWNER AND BAR OPERATOR
GIN & BEER

What started out as an obsessive hobby for husband-and-wife team Steve and Gemma Wheeler developed into opening their own venue. Nestled in a railway arch in the up-and-coming neighborhood of Deptford, the bar specializes in superb cocktails made with, as you can guess by the name, gin and beer.

YOU OPENED YOUR OWN VENUE WITHOUT ANY PREVIOUS HOSPITALITY OR BAR EXPERIENCE?
My background in cocktails before we opened this place was that I like to drink cocktails, and I like to make them, and I like getting creative when I do so.

We did gin nights and cocktail nights with friends at home and people started saying, "This is getting out of hand; you really should be charging for this." We called the whole operation "Paddy's Pub," because that's what the bar is called in *It's Always Sunny in Philadelphia*.

I'm completely self-taught, just from running my little hobby bar in the garden. I'm not from the industry at all. I approach it in the same way as food. You can make a quick drink out of store/cupboard ingredients, or you can make an incredible drink with great ingredients from scratch—and with a bit of love—and it will be unbelievable. That's how I approach it.

I do like gin, but also I love beer, especially craft beer. My brothers all live in South London, and we'd get together to drink beers. From there we'd go to a gin bar—with my brothers drinking the only beer in the place. My idea here was to take two things and do them well and in the process attract two different demographics: beer lovers and gin lovers.

Gin is the most versatile spirit. Beer is the most versatile drink. So you can really get creative with the categories. All our cocktails are made with gin and beer as well.

IS YOUR CLIENTELE LOCAL OR ARE YOU AIMING TO BECOME A DESTINATION BAR FOR GIN AND BEER LOVERS?

We're aiming to become a destination bar. We've had a few people travel here. For example, there was a Negroni club that came through from West London and they saw it as a bit of an adventure.

We've found that beer people are more willing to travel than cocktail people at the moment. That said, there are tons of cocktail establishments in the center of the city, but not many places that serve Belgian beer. We get a few locals but, on the weekends, it's people that have traveled to visit us.

I think beer is an underutilized ingredient in cocktails, though. It works as both a souring and as a sweetening agent, or even as a lengthener. It's so versatile. I'd love to see it used more in drinks, especially with the explosion of the craft beer scene.

– BAIJIU –

An Asian-inspired take on the Bijou cocktail originally created by the father of modern bartending, Harry Johnson. Assistant head mixologist Davide Cironelli introduces intense citrus that gives way to earthy and herbaceous notes. The ROKU Gin from Japan and Hong Kong Baijiu (which is actually produced in China and Italy) contribute both subtlety and strength.

GLASSWARE: Large snifter

GARNISH: None

- ⅞ oz. Suntory ROKU Gin
- 1 oz. Carpano Antica Formula Vermouth
- 2 teaspoons Green Chartreuse
- 1 teaspoon Hong Kong Baijiu
- ½ teaspoon Campari
- 2 drops citric acid
- 3 dashes orange bitters

1. Chill the snifter.

2. Add all of the ingredients to a cocktail shaker filled with ice and shake vigorously until chilled.

3. Place a block of ice in the snifter and double-strain the cocktail over the ice.

- CAPTAIN AWESOME -

General manager Katrina Nahtmane came up with an early itera-tion of this drink as a young bartender, only to see it stolen by the bar owner, who didn't credit her for its creation—even after she left the bar. She then perfected the recipe and named it after her former boss's habit of talking about how great he was.

GLASSWARE: Rocks glass
GARNISH: Cucumber slice

- 2 cucumber slices
- 1 oz. Beefeater London Dry gin
- 1 oz. fresh lemon juice
- ½ oz. Ancho Reyes liqueur
- ½ oz. Mahiki coconut rum liqueur
- ½ oz. Simple Syrup (see page 24)
- 1 oz. pineapple juice

1. Add the cucumber slices to a cocktail shaker and muddle.

2. Add ice and the remaining ingredients and shake vigorously until chilled.

3. Double-strain into a rocks glass containing one large ice cube.

4. Garnish with a slice of cucumber.

SEVEN AT BRIXTON

7 MARKET ROW, BRIXTON
LONDON SW9 8LB

- GINGER BEER & BASIL MOJITO -

First created in 2011, Liam Brown livens up a Mojito with tangy flavors that keep it fresh and fizzy rather than minty and subdued. Replacing the traditional mint with basil adds a pleasant zing, as well.

GLASSWARE: Highball glass

GARNISH: None

- 5 lime wedges
- 1 teaspoon caster sugar
- 5 basil leaves
- 1¾ oz. white rum
- 1¾ oz. ginger beer

1. Place the lime wedges and caster sugar in the highball glass and muddle.

2. Slap the basil leaves to release their aromatics and add them to the glass.

3. Fill the glass with crushed ice and then add the rum and ginger beer.

4. Stir until chilled and top up the cocktail with more crushed ice.

– BUTTERED RUM –

Chief booze engineer Patrick Hobbs is rightfully proud of his delicious Buttered Rum, a wonderfully rich and syrupy concoction. What's more, any leftover butter solids can be used to make more Buttered Rum. They're also perfect for apple pie.

GLASSWARE: Rocks glass
GARNISH: Orange slice

- **9 oz. quality unsalted butter**
- **1¾ oz. demerara sugar**
- **2 vanilla bean pods**
- **½ star anise pod**
- **½ oz. Angostura Bitters**
- **1 750 ml bottle Appleton Estate Signature Blend rum (or preferred Jamaican rum)**

1. Place the butter in a saucepan and melt over medium-high heat.

2. Add the sugar and stir until it has dissolved.

3. Split the vanilla pods open and add them to the pan along with the star anise and bitters.

4. Add the rum and reduce heat so that the rum gets gently infused.

5. Remove the pan from heat and let the mixture cool.

6. Cover and refrigerate overnight.

7. Remove the layer of butter solids that have collected on the surface the next day.

8. Strain through cheesecloth back into the bottle of rum, pour over ice into the rocks glass, and garnish with an orange slice. Store the bottled cocktail in the refrigerator when not in use.

SHRUB AND SHUTTER

336 COLDHARBOUR LANE, BRIXTON
LONDON SW9 8QH

- JIRO DREAMS OF SUSHI -

Named after Japanese sushi master Jiro Ono and the documentary about his life and work, this cocktail is ideally served alongside mackerel sashimi to provide the proper experience. The sweet sake will do battle with the bitter sharpness of the wasabi tincture, creating a thoroughly enjoyable balance.

GLASSWARE: Ceramic mug
GARNISH: Shiso leaf

- 1⅜ oz. Ki No Bi Kyoto Dry Gin
- ¾ oz. Akashi-Tai Daiginjo sake
- 2 teaspoons Miso Shrub
- 3 drops Wasabi Tincture
- Lemon oil, to mist
- 1 piece mackerel sashimi
- Soy sauce, to taste

1. Add the gin, sake, and shrub to a ceramic mug and stir to combine.

2. Add the Wasabi Tincture and mist the lemon oil over the top.

3. Use a brush to coat the mackerel sashimi with soy sauce. Garnish the cocktail with the shiso leaf and serve the sashimi on the side.

MISO SHRUB (MAKES 35 OZ.): Place 10½ oz. water, 10½ oz. white wine vinegar, 10 ½ oz. sugar, and 3½ oz. white miso paste in a saucepan and warm over high heat, stirring until everything has dissolved. Remove from heat and let cool before using or storing.

WASABI TINCTURE: Place ¾ oz. freshly grated wasabi, 1 teaspoon wasabi paste, and 7 oz. of 88 percent spirit (Shrub and Shutter uses Balkan 176° Vodka) in a mason jar and stir to combine. Strain before using or storing. Some of this tincture would be lovely mixed into the soy sauce used on the mackerel sashimi.

THREE EIGHT FOUR

384 COLDHARBOUR LANE, BRIXTON, LONDON SW9 8LF

- ZIGGY STARDUST -

The Three Eight Four team wanted to create something both local to Brixton and to have a drink featuring edible glitter on the menu. Johnny Rushton conceived of a drink that ticks both boxes, and honors Brixton native David Bowie. Combining a Cosmopolitan with a Martini, the result is quite vibrant, and different from either of those standards.

GLASSWARE: Cocktail glass
GARNISH: Edible pink glitter

- 1¾ oz. Lemon-Infused Vodka
- 2 teaspoons crème de cassis
- 1¾ oz. pomegranate juice
- ½ oz. fresh lemon juice
- 1 egg white

1. Add all of the ingredients to a cocktail shaker containing no ice and dry shake for 15 seconds. Add ice and shake vigorously until chilled.

2. Strain into the cocktail glass.

3. Garnish with edible pink glitter, in the shape of the iconic Aladdin Sane lightning bolt.

LEMON-INFUSED VODKA: Peel 1 lemon, place the peel in a mason jar filled with vodka (or directly in the bottle of vodka), and let steep for 24 to 36 hours. Strain before using or storing.

EAST LONDON

THE TUESDAY CLUB • MARLOWE •

UNSCALPE • NIGHT BLAZE • SHINTO

DAISY • CHARCOAL OLD FASHIONED •

PIÑA FUMADA • I NEED A KYRÖ •

CHAMPAGNE PALOMA • WHERE THE

F*CK IS FRANK • GOOD FORTUNE •

KANJI IN THE EVENING • MOMBAI MULE

• MEZCAL SURVIVOR • CHINOTTO

NEGRONI • MÓRIARTY • TWO IRISHMEN

I n the past, East London housed many of the city's poorest communities and manufacturing areas. Successive waves of immigrants from around the world landed here in their search for opportunities and a better life. These days, East London is a bustling microcosm of the city, including its rough edges. It features vibrant, multicultural neighborhoods and historical tourist sites such as the Tower of London. Canary Wharf is a center of global finance. Sections like Hackney and Shoreditch have evolved into hip cultural hubs with plenty of bars and clubs full of eager revelers.

It is also easy to find a good drink here—whether you're in the mood for luxurious establishments catering to high finance types, seedy dive bars, classy bistros, or traditional pubs.

BEHIND THIS WALL

411 MARE STREET, LONDON E8 1HY

– THE TUESDAY CLUB –

This is essentially founder Alex Harris's rum Old Fashioned enhanced with some nifty ingredients, including Behind This Wall's banana-and-CBD oil syrup, which can be bought online. Where a traditional Old Fashioned is soft and sweet with vanilla emerging from the bourbon, this element gets cranked up here thanks to the rum, in addition to soft fruits and spices.

GLASSWARE: Rocks glass
GARNISH: Dehydrated banana chip

- **3 dashes cinnamon bitters (Bittermens 'Elemakule Tiki Bitters preferred)**
- **1¼ oz. light rum (El Dorado 3-Year-Old preferred)**
- **¾ oz. spiced rum (Drum & Black preferred)**
- **¼ oz. Behind This Wall Banana CBD Syrup (alternately, use banana syrup with a drop or two of CBD oil)**
- **Pear Calvados, to mist**

1. Add the bitters, rums, and a large block of ice to a rocks glass.

2. Add the syrup and stir until chilled.

3. Top with one spray of Pear Calvados mist (place an atomizer on the bottle or pour a bit of Calvados into a spray bottle) and garnish with the dehydrated banana chip.

This is Alex Harris's take on a Gimlet. The St-Germain and cucumber will complement but not overwhelm the gin or the citrus from the lime, while adding a flowery tang and refreshing element, respectively.

GLASSWARE: Embassy sour glass
GARNISH: None

- **6 thin cucumber slices**
- **¼ oz. fresh lime juice**

- **1½ oz. Hendrick's Midsummer Solstice gin (or any aromatic London Dry)**
- **1½ oz. St-Germain**

1. Chill the embassy sour glass and set aside.

2. Muddle the cucumber slices and lime juice in a cocktail shaker, add the remaining ingredients, fill the shaker with ice, shake vigorously until chilled, and strain into the chilled glass.

BOKAN

40 MARSH WALL, ISLE OF DOGS, LONDON E14 9TP

– UNSCALPE –

The Unscalpe follows a fairly typical bittersweet blueprint for an aperitivo cocktail. However, this one, created by head bartender Slawomir Wrzeszcz, has a subtle, smoky twist, courtesy of the mezcal and the unique Islay Cask bitters. For Wrzeszcz, "It strikes the perfect balance between the sunny day and the dark night."

GLASSWARE: Goblet
GARNISH: Strip of orange peel

- 1½ oz. mezcal
- 1 oz. Kamm & Sons Islay Cask
- 1 oz. Aperol

1. Add the ingredients to a mixing glass filled with ice, stir until chilled, and strain into the goblet.

2. Garnish with the strip of orange peel.

– NIGHT BLAZE –

The smoke in this cocktail will be surprisingly subtle as Slawomir Wrzeszcz's objective is to ensure the Ardbeg gets all over the glass before everything else goes in. If done correctly, the rich fruits from the Glenmorangie and the plum sake will be followed by a lovely finish that features the aforementioned smoke and long, dry, herbal notes.

GLASSWARE: Goblet
GARNISH: Dark chocolate or walnuts, served on the side

- ½ teaspoon Ardbeg 10-Year-Old (another strong peated whisky will work)
- 1¾ oz. Glenmorangie The Quinta Ruban
- ⅞ oz. plum sake
- ¼ oz. Noilly Prat Dry Vermouth
- 1 teaspoon Green Chartreuse

1. Rinse the goblet with the Ardbeg.

2. Combine the remaining ingredients in a mixing glass filled with ice, stir until chilled, and strain into the goblet.

3. Serve with dark chocolate or walnuts on the side.

BULL IN A CHINA SHOP

196 SHOREDITCH HIGH STREET, SHOREDITCH
LONDON E1 6LG

- SHINTO DAISY -

Bar manager Paul Loki created this whisky-based cocktail that a non-whisky drinker likely would enjoy, and it doubles as a gateway to other whisky-based drinks. It's refreshing, and also allows the primary spirit to shine without being overwhelming. It balances fruity, sweet, and sour flavors. Feel free to adjust the sweetness by adding more syrup.

GLASSWARE: Glencairn glass

GARNISH: Edible flowers

- 1¼ oz. Mars Kasei Whisky
- ⅞ oz. fresh lemon juice
- ⅞ oz. plum sake
- 1¾ teaspoons gomme syrup or Simple Syrup (see page 24)

- 8 dashes Peychaud's Bitters
- 3 dashes Ms. Better's Bitters Miraculous Foamer or 1 egg white

1. Add all of the ingredients to a cocktail shaker containing no ice and dry shake for 15 seconds.

2. Add ice to the shaker, shake vigorously until chilled, and strain over two ice cubes into a Glencairn glass.

3. Garnish with the edible flowers.

– CHARCOAL OLD FASHIONED –

Following a suggestion to use activated charcoal on the food menu to make Bull in a China Shop's burger buns jet black in color (and also to provide a healthy kick), Christian Cuevas then used it as part of a unique twist on an Old Fashioned. The result is light and floral, though the optional pipette of Lapsang-infused Nikka whisky will add a smoky hit as well.

GLASSWARE: Rocks glass
GARNISH: Orange twist, stirring stick,
and (optional) pipette of Tea-Infused Whisky

- 1¾ oz. Tea-Infused Whisky
- 2 teaspoons Chamomile Syrup
- ½ teaspoon activated charcoal powder
- 1 dash Angostura Bitters
- 1 dash orange bitters

1. Place all of the ingredients in a mixing glass filled with ice, stir until chilled, and strain into a rocks glass filled with ice.

2. Garnish with an orange twist, a stirring stick, and, if using, add a pipette filled with the Tea-Infused Whisky.

TEA-INFUSED WHISKY: Place ⅜ oz. loose-leaf Lapsang souchong tea in a 750 ml bottle of Nikka From the Barrel Whisky and let it steep for 45 minutes. Strain before using or storing.

CHAMOMILE SYRUP (MAKES 35 OZ.): In a saucepan, boil 2¾ cups water and then add 1 oz. loose-leaf chamomile tea and remove the pan from heat; let it steep for 1 hour. Strain tea into a clean saucepan, add 3⅓ lbs. caster sugar, and simmer, while stirring, until the sugar has dissolved. Let syrup cool completely before using or storing.

DISCOUNT SUIT COMPANY

29A WENTWORTH
STREET, SPITALFIELDS
LONDON E1 7TB

– PIÑA FUMADA –

The Piña Fumada was created by Discount Suit Company's director, Andy Kerr, during the bar's first year in business and quickly became a firm favorite. The cocktail is sharp, smoky, honey sweet, and very unique in overall flavor, putting a refreshing tiki twist on a Mexican staple.

GLASSWARE: Highball glass
GARNISH: Crushed ice, pineapple leaf, and lemon wedge

- 1¼ oz. Quiquiriqui Mezcal
- ¾ oz. fresh lemon juice
- 2 teaspoons Velvet Falernum
- ½ oz. honey
- Club soda, to top

1. Add all of the ingredients, except the club soda, to a cocktail shaker filled with ice, shake vigorously until chilled, and strain into a highball glass filled with ice.

2. Top with the club soda and garnish with the crushed ice, pineapple leaf, and lemon wedge.

BAR BANTER
ANDY KERR, CO-FOUNDER
AND OPERATIONS DIRECTOR
DISCOUNT SUIT COMPANY

He may have started his career collecting glasses when he was 17, but a now-mature Andy Kerr likes to have his fingers in many pies. Not only does he run two top-quality London bars and a hotel in Mexico, he also produces a podcast about music and drinks.

COULD YOU TELL ME ABOUT THE DISCOUNT SUIT COMPANY AND THE SUN TAVERN?

I always wanted to do my own project and during my travels I met two guys who I connected well with. We always wanted to do something since, even though we'd never worked together. Then we had the opportunity to start the Discount Suit Company and we went from there. We invested all the money we ever had in the world to see what would happen, and it's been super successful. We launched that in early 2015 and then nine months later we did the Sun Tavern.

The Discount Suit Company is classically inspired, working with forgotten classic cocktails and Northern Soul music. It's really gritty but with an amazing environment. With the Sun Tavern, I used to work in a lot of whisky bars and I saw the emergence of Irish whiskey coming again. So, I really wanted to include that within a concept that used craft beers as well as classic cocktails. Someone once described it as "what pubs will be like in 20 years." You know you get this style more in America, where you can go in a pub and get a Martini, but it just doesn't really exist in our culture. So, we're doing something like that, with the Irish whiskey element.

COULD YOU TELL ME MORE ABOUT THE DSC APPROACH TO COCKTAILS?

When we set up, the original concept was forgotten classic cocktails. I used to read a lot of old, original books so I was picking out these classic cocktails that people didn't know.

At the time, there weren't a lot of bars really doing it at the level that we were. What we serve is based around classic cocktails that are not as well known as everyone thinks, covering drinks from the late 1800s to the present day.

We're using just three-to-four ingredient cocktails. Super-simple, super-boozy, and accessible to everyone. We use spirits from all around the world, using only interesting things to make really delicious drinks.

HOW HAS THE APPROACH TO COCKTAILS CHANGED IN LONDON OVER THE LAST FEW YEARS?

I think that the major change is the consumer knowledge now.

We as bartenders always have had interest in flavor profiles and spirits. Now the customer demands so much more and that's pushed things. In the old days, it was like talking to a brick wall. If you talked about flavors they'd just stop listening. They'd say, 'Oh, just give me a Mojito.' Now people are coming in looking for specific styles of cocktails or flavors.

I think it's great for the industry. It's developed in a similar way to food. I think it'll still be even more refined in the future as well. I mean, even nowadays you can go to a pub and get a great Gin & Tonic and a great Bloody Mary. Ten years ago, you couldn't do that. Nowadays there's so many more options. This has been the biggest change that I've observed.

THE FAT BEAR

61 CARTER LANE, LONDON EC4V 5DY

– I NEED A KYRŌ –
(AKA CHOCOLATE CHIP FINNISH FLIP)

Developed for the Kyrö Extemporye cocktail competition, the bar's co-founder, Gareth Rees, was looking to make something fun, subversive, and delicious. The punchy, rye-based gin gives a really firm backbone to this cocktail, which has the central goal of evoking a banana milkshake, albeit significantly updated for adulthood.

GLASSWARE: Large coupe

GARNISH: Freshly grated nutmeg

- 1½ oz. Kyrö Napue Gin
- ⅞ oz. Tempus Fugit Crème de Banane
- ½ oz. Tempus Fugit Crème de Cacao
- ¾ oz. double cream
- 1 egg
- 6 drops Ms. Better's Bitters Chocolate

1. Add all of the ingredients to a cocktail shaker filled with ice, shake vigorously until chilled, and double-strain into the large coupe.

2. Garnish with freshly grated nutmeg.

BAR BANTER
GARETH REES, OWNER AND DOGSBODY, THE FAT BEAR

Gareth Rees had an unconventional career before opening The Fat Bear. He was a consultant, a professional poker player, and also worked at tech start-ups before he found his true calling. Now he runs the bar and his wife, Judy, runs the kitchen of their award-winning restaurant.

WHAT MAKES YOUR COCKTAIL LIST SPECIAL COMPARED TO OTHER LONDON BARS?

I learned my way around drinks from people who preferred to take old classics and slightly reinterpret or improve them, and sometimes doing stuff a little more off the deep end. It's how I do things, too.

I also like to tiki-fy drinks, bringing in some playful, Polynesian nonsense when I can. And I really love doing flips, which I think don't get enough attention. But they are actually really old school. There are some ancient recipes that are essentially flips, going back hundreds of years, using eggnog and things like that. It's fun exploring things that are a little abstruse, but not gimmicky, and that's what we try to do here.

The cocktail menu is also pretty whiskey-heavy—maybe 60 percent of the menu involves American whiskey and I love rye whiskey, too. There's always a Sazerac of some kind in there and variations on a Manhattan. We have a strong American influence here, especially as my wife's a New Yorker, and I've learned a lot from visiting the city and drinking there as a happy punter.

BEING LOCATED IN THE CENTRAL BUSINESS DISTRICT OF LONDON, I'M ASSUMING YOU GET A LOT OF BOOZY BANKERS AS YOUR CLIENTELE?

I think we've been very fortunate in that we get a lot of self-selection. So, we don't get a lot of the archetypal big, brash city workers throwing tons of cash around [during] big, boozy lunches. I think the culture in the air has changed a lot, anyways, so that's less common, too.

We've found that the nice people in the area find out about us and keep coming. They tell their friends and create a virtuous circle of decent, low-key, easy customers, which is not what you'd expect of the area.

I've heard from many of our regulars that we're kind of a little getaway for them because you can come here and cloister yourself from the bustle outside or be a safe haven away from the furnace of the investment bank.

We also get lots of business travelers, and many returning American tourists. There was a guy in here recently who comes in three or four times a year, typically every single time he's in town, and he always stays at a nearby hotel. People like using us as a base, especially as around here there is a lot of food-chain mediocrity.

HOW DO YOU THINK BREXIT IS GOING TO AFFECT BUSINESS?

I'm concerned around the supply chain and the disruptions Brexit might bring. Perishable foods are particularly problematic, but perishable drinks are also difficult. You know the majority of the whiskey and our wine all comes from overseas. And with currency being as volatile as it is at the moment, you know if we drop to 1.1 to the dollar or parity then everything goes up 20 percent.

It's all well and good if you just go and put up your prices 20 percent. But in an environment where disposable income is more limited, fewer people will be wanting to go out and go drinking. I think that's the most immediate existential threat to us and to most hospitality businesses.

HACHA

378 KINGSLAND ROAD
DALSTON, LONDON E8 4AA

– CHAMPAGNE PALOMA –

Massively popular in Mexico, the Paloma is a relatively simple cocktail, consisting of tequila and grapefruit soda. This is a delicious sparkling variation, with founder Deano Moncrieffe drawing on his experience as a brand ambassador for Don Julio.

GLASSWARE: Champagne flute

GARNISH: Grapefruit twist

- ¾ oz. Don Julio Tequila
- 2½ oz. pink-and-white grapefruit juice blend (1:1 ratio)
- 1 dash Cinnamon Syrup
- Champagne or sparkling wine, to top

1. Add all of the ingredients, except for the Champagne or sparkling wine, to a champagne flute and stir.

2. Top with Champagne or sparkling wine and garnish with the grapefruit twist.

CINNAMON SYRUP: Add 4 cinnamon sticks to a basic Simple Syrup (see page 24) after the sugar has dissolved, and let them steep as the mixture cools. Remove the cinnamon sticks before using or storing.

BAR BANTER
DEANO MONCRIEFFE
FOUNDER AND DIRECTOR, HACHA

Deano Moncrieffe's new bar, Hacha, is out to make the incredible world of agave spirits accessible to anyone. Rather than feature hundreds of drinks, the longtime brand ambassador has narrowed the selection to 25 choices, a living collection that he actively changes and curates over time.

WHERE ARE YOU FROM AND HOW DID YOU END UP IN LONDON?
Originally, I'm from Birmingham and ended up in London after working as a bartender across Europe. I first worked at a cocktail bar in Paris called the Chesterfield Cafe, where my mixology education began. When I came back to the UK, I lived in Brighton for 10 years and commuted to London on a regular basis for work before moving here permanently around 12 years ago.

WHAT MAKES HACHA STAND OUT COMPARED TO OTHER LONDON BARS? WHY IS YOUR BABY BEAUTIFUL?
I've been specializing in agave spirits for over a decade. I travel all over the world as a brand ambassador for Don Julio, and I've always had a desire to make agave spirits more accessible.

At Hacha I wanted to make agave spirits more approachable and simplify what can be a confusing category for new consumers. Unlike most bars in London, we have a constantly evolving back bar of only 25 agave spirits. As soon as a bottle is finished I will replace it with something new and different.

We also wanted to move away from the traditional Mexican decor that you find here that tends to be very bright and often cluttered. My partner, Emma, did all the design and reflected the simplicity of the cocktails with a stripped-back design that features playful Mexican artwork, Mexican textures and materials, and an agave-inspired color palette. It's a beautiful and calm space that you want to spend the whole evening in.

HOW DO YOU MAKE AGAVE SPIRITS STAND OUT HERE?

My style is very much based on creating cocktails that are clean and uncomplicated in appearance but have hidden layers of flavor. I want them to be familiar in name but different in taste and expectation.

Everything on the back bar is served with a flavor enhancer that matches perfectly with the individual spirit and helps to bring out another layer of the agave spirit. I literally tried hundreds of different flavor enhancers with different agave spirits when I was creating the concept. I wanted it to be fun so what you will see is quite unusual with the enhancers. We have everything from mezcal served with milky bar buttons, Pechuga Mezcal with beef Monster Munch crisps, tequila with char-grilled pineapple soaked in rum, and a Raicilla served with CBD oil.

WHAT HAVE BEEN THE ADVANTAGES AND DISADVANTAGES TO OWNING YOUR OWN COCKTAIL BAR IN LONDON?

When you open a bar for the first time you realize just how little support small businesses are given by the government. There is very little incentive for new entrepreneurs who want to do their own thing. Every new business is a gamble and a risk, especially if you are doing something completely different to what's been done before. I have so much respect for everyone who opens a bar and has their own premises. That's enough moaning and negativity from me.

The advantages of opening a bar in London are that you do have a very receptive customer demographic keen to try new things. Bartenders here support each other a lot, trade friends and colleagues support each other a lot. When we opened there was such a great level of genuine love and wanting us to do well that I will never forget it.

LOOKING GLASS
COCKTAIL CLUB

49 HACKNEY ROAD
LONDON E2 7NX

– WHERE THE F*CK IS FRANK –

Part of the Looking Glass Cocktail Club's Music and Cocktail menu, creator Giacomo Apolloni recommends drinking this to Frank Sinatra's version of "Forget Domani" (*domani* means "tomorrow" in Italian). This Mediterranean twist on a Manhattan nods to Ol' Blue Eyes's roots with Italian-inflected ingredients: dried tomatoes, olive oil, and basil.

GLASSWARE: Coupette

GARNISH: None

- 1½ oz. Sun-Dried Tomato-Infused Grappa, washed with olive oil
- ¾ oz. Basil-Infused Gentian Wine
- 1¾ teaspoons Green Chartreuse
- ¾ teaspoon Cynar
- 2 drops Bitter Bastards Naga Chilli Bitters

1. Add all of the ingredients to a mixing glass filled with ice, stir until chilled, and strain into the coupette.

SUN-DRIED TOMATO-INFUSED GRAPPA: There are two options: the preferred option is to place a 750 ml bottle of Grappa Nardini Bianca and 5½ oz. sun-dried tomatoes in a vacuum bag and cook sous vide for 2 hours at 150°F. The other option is to place the bottle of grappa and sun-dried tomatoes in a mason jar and refrigerate for 5 days. Strain before using or storing.

OLIVE OIL WASH: Combine the infused grappa and 2 oz. extra virgin olive oil in a container with a lid. Shake vigorously and store in a cool, dark place for 24 hours. Place the container in the freezer until the olive oil completely separates and solidifies. Remove the olive oil layer, then strain the grappa through a coffee filter to clarify.

BASIL-INFUSED GENTIAN WINE: Combine a 750 ml bottle of gentian wine, like Suze, and 10 basil leaves in a jar and refrigerate for 4 hours. Strain before using or storing.

KYM'S

19 BLOOMBERG
ARCADE, LONDON
EC4N 8AR

– GOOD FORTUNE –

The inspiration for this drink created by founder Andrew Wong comes from the Mandarin word for "gold," which sounds the same as the word for "tangerine." Oranges and tangerines, therefore, are often seen as symbols of wealth, health, and good fortune in Chinese culture. The acidity of the yuzu and lime blends elegantly with the smoky sweetness of the Zacapa rum, and the touch of heat from the Vanilla & Chili Syrup really rounds off the whole drink.

GLASSWARE: Cocktail glass
GARNISH: Torched Orange Twist

- 1⅜ oz. Ron Zacapa rum
- ¾ oz. Akashi-Tai Umeshu Sake
- 2 teaspoons Chinese Orange Marmalade
- 1 oz. fresh lime juice
- ½ oz. Vanilla & Chili Syrup

1. Chill the cocktail glass.

2. Add all of the ingredients to a cocktail shaker filled with ice, shake vigorously until chilled, and double-strain into the chilled cocktail glass.

3. Garnish with the Torched Orange Twist.

CHINESE ORANGE MARMALADE: Wash and dry 20 oranges, halve them, remove the seeds, and slice the oranges into thin slivers that include the peel. Place the orange slices in a saucepan, add enough water to cover them, and bring to a boil; maintain rolling boil for 8 minutes and then lower the heat so that the mixture simmers. Stir in sugar to taste and continue to cook until the water has evaporated. Stick a spoon into the cooked oranges; if the back of the spoon comes out sticky, the marmalade is ready. Add 1 tablespoon of yuzu juice as a preservative and store in an airtight container.

VANILLA & CHILI SYRUP (MAKES 1½ CUPS): Place 2 cups caster sugar and 1 cup water in a saucepan and cook over low heat, while stirring, until the sugar dissolves. Add 2 jalapeño peppers and 4 vanilla beans to the mixture and stir to incorporate. Stir in another cup of caster sugar and continue stirring until it dissolves, making sure not to let the syrup come to a boil. Remove from heat, let cool, and strain before using or storing.

TORCHED ORANGE TWIST: Cut a rounded slice of orange peel, at least 1 inch in diameter. It's not a problem if it gets some of the pith; a thick peel is fine. Hold the strip of orange peel about 2 inches above a lit match for a couple seconds. Twist and squeeze the peel over the lit match, while holding it above the cocktail. If desired, rub the torched peel around the rim of the glass. Drop the twist into the drink or discard.

MAP MAISON

321 KINGSLAND ROAD, DALSTON
LONDON E8 4DL

– KANJI IN THE EVENING –

The meticulous attention to detail that is synonymous with Japan inspired both the flavor and visual design of this cocktail created by general manager Heidi Kampa. Here, the slightly peaty Hakushu Distillers Reserve whisky gets a fruity lift combined with soft spice and citrus, creating an exciting balance of flavors. If you have one, use a smoke gun to add a fragrant cherrywood aroma to a mix—the smoke also looks mighty classy.

GLASSWARE: Rocks glass

GARNISH: None

- 1¾ oz. Hakushu Distillers Reserve whisky
- 1¾ teaspoons Yellow Chartreuse
- ½ oz. Aperol
- ½ oz. Pink Pepper-and-Pomegranate Syrup
- ¾ oz. fresh lime juice

1. Add all of the ingredients to a cocktail shaker filled with ice, shake vigorously until chilled, and double-strain over an ice sphere into a rocks glass.

2. If desired, use a smoke gun filled with cherrywood chips to smoke the drink; don't leave it running too long: 10 to 15 seconds is about right.

PINK PEPPER-AND-POMEGRANATE SYRUP: In a saucepan, combine 8 cups pomegranate juice, ½ cup sugar, ¼ cup fresh lemon juice, and 4 teaspoons pink peppercorns and bring to a boil. Lower heat and simmer for 30 minutes, remove from heat, and let cool. Strain before using or storing.

– MOMBAI MULE –

ondon's Fogg bars are inspired by the adventures of Phileas Fogg from Jules Verne's *Around the World in 80 Days*. At Mrs. Fogg's, the inspiration comes from his wife, the Indian princess Aouda. As a result, the cocktail menu is Indian-themed. Here, Grazia Russo gives the Moscow Mule an Indian makeover, using cardamom and cinnamon.

GLASSWARE: Moscow Mule mug
GARNISH: Bunch of curly parsley, dehydrated pear slice, and confectioners' sugar

- 1¾ oz. Cardamom-Infused Russian Standard Vodka
- 1¾ oz. apple juice
- ⅞ oz. pear puree
- ½ oz. fresh lime juice
- 1¾ teaspoons Cinnamon Syrup (see page 249)
- Fentimans Ginger Beer, to top

1. Build the drink in a mule mug filled with ice and stir until chilled.

2. Garnish with the bunch of curly parsley, dehydrated pear slice, and confectioners' sugar.

CARDAMOM-INFUSED RUSSIAN STANDARD VODKA: Place 10 green cardamom pods and 750 ml Russian Standard Vodka in a vacuum bag and cook it sous vide at 134.6°F for 2 hours. Alternately, you can steep the cardamom pods in the vodka for 2 weeks, storing in a cool, dark place and shaking every few days. Strain before using or storing.

- MEZCAL SURVIVOR -

Bar manager Omar Valadez created this cocktail based on his favorite flavors: citrus, candy-like sweetness, and smoke. Add the flamed absinthe on top and a few maraschino cherries and you end up with a wonderfully balanced concoction. You'll feel the smokiness of the mezcal, but it interacts nicely with all the other ingredients.

GLASSWARE: Cocktail glass
GARNISH: 3 maraschino cherries

- 1¾ oz. Montelobos Mezcal
- ⅞ oz. Cocchi Americano Bianco
- ¾ oz. Lime Syrup
- ⅞ oz. fresh lemon juice
- Absinthe, to mist

1. Combine all of the ingredients, except for the absinthe, in a cocktail shaker filled with ice, shake vigorously, and strain into the cocktail glass.

2. Spray the absinthe over the drink. If desired, light it on fire and then garnish with the 3 maraschino cherries speared on a toothpick.

LIME SYRUP: Make a Rich Simple Syrup (see page 24). After the sugar has dissolved, add the zest of 1 lime for every 4 oz. of produced syrup, and the same amount of lime juice as the water initially used. Let steep for 15 minutes, strain, and refrigerate for 1 hour before using.

SAGER + WILDE

250 PARADISE ROW, CAMBRIDGE
HEATH, LONDON E2 9LE

— CHINOTTO NEGRONI —

Sager + Wilde focuses on reimagining classic cocktails and celebrating Italian cocktail culture's intimate relationship with food. With this Negroni variation by Marcis Dzelzainis, an extra bit of bitterness from the liqueur and added brightness from the lemon juice results in a crisp and drinkable variation on the old favorite.

GLASSWARE: Rocks glass
GARNISH: Orange twist

- ⅞ oz. Beefeater Gin
- ⅞ oz. Campari
- ½ oz. Carpano Rosso Classico
- ½ oz. Quaglia Chinotto Liqueur
- 1 teaspoon fresh lemon juice

1. Add all of the ingredients to a mixing glass filled with ice, stir until chilled, and strain over ice into a rocks glass.

2. Garnish with the orange twist.

- MÓRIARTY -

Ophie Del Vecchio's Móriarty is a fascinating combination of a standard and White Negroni, plus the unique flavor of Picon Amer. If you think you can handle its strong and bitter flavors, this might be the drink for you.

GLASSWARE: Coupe

GARNISH: Strip of orange peel

- ⅞ oz. Mór Irish Gin
- 2 teaspoons Victory Gin
- ¾ oz. Cocchi Di Torino
- 2 teaspoons Suze
- 1 teaspoon Picon Amer
- 2 dashes Angostura Bitters

1. Chill the coupe.

2. Add all of the ingredients to a mixing glass filled with ice, stir until chilled, and strain into the chilled coupe.

3. Garnish with the strip of orange peel.

THE SUN TAVERN
441 BETHNAL GREEN ROAD
BETHNAL GREEN
LONDON E2 0AN

As a bar specializing in Irish whiskey, it makes sense to have an Irish whiskey cocktail on the menu. The Two Irishmen is bar director Andy Kerr's twist on a Manhattan, with complexity added by the Bénédictine to complement the creamy, vanilla-forward flavor of the whiskey.

GLASSWARE: Cocktail glass

GARNISH: Lemon twist

- 1¼ oz. Tyrconnell Whiskey
- 2 teaspoons Bénédictine
- ¾ oz. Cocchi Americano Vermouth
- 2 dashes Peychaud's Bitters

1. Add all of the ingredients to a mixing glass filled with ice, stir until chilled, and strain into the cocktail glass.

2. Garnish with the lemon twist.

BEST OF THE BEST

THE JEROME • CONNAUGHT MARTINI •

DIABLO OTOÑO • FAM MARGARITA •

I WILL SURVIVE • DALKULLA •

MIND MAPS • PICCOLINA •

PALO SANTO GIMLET • SHISO MISO

One of the questions I asked in the many interviews I conducted for this book was: "Which bars in London are doing something special with cocktails?"

Each response listed numerous bars, but specific names appeared again and again. Some of the selections here, including the American Bar at The Savoy and The Connaught Bar, are not surprising—they are renowned, award-winning London institutions. Some newer bars, such as Lyaness and Tayēr + Elementary, boast serious pedigrees of experienced founders known and respected by the global drinks industry. Others here wouldn't pass for more than a small hole in the wall, yet they have created magic in their drinks.

Whatever their size, history, decor, or provenance, they all share a profound dedication to providing spectacular cocktails and service to their patrons.

AMERICAN BAR AT THE SAVOY

THE SAVOY, STRAND, LONDON WC2R 0EZ

This is simply one of the best bars in the world. Don't believe me? Ask any of London's top bartenders. One of London's true drinks institutions, it is the source of some of the world's best-known classic cocktails. Serving drinks for more than 125 years, many of the world's most-famous figures have hung out (and sometimes drunk themselves into a stupor) here, with photos on the wall serving as memorials to those illustrious, and infamous, visitors.

While the bar is a classy, Art Deco joint and always busy, the glitz is not over the top—although you should expect to pay top pound for the world-class drinks—with live jazz piano setting the mood every evening.

Maxim Schulte, a German, currently holds the position of head bartender at the American Bar—the 11th one in the bar's history—an honor bestowed after he ran the bar at the Ritz-Carlton in Macau, China. He follows in the footsteps of distinguished predecessors Ada Coleman (see page 38) and Harry Craddock (see page 41), among others, and is aware of the weighty legacy he is charged with maintaining: "The American Bar is a very historical place, but also, in these modern times, it is wonderful and vibrant. Every day brings amazing new people into the bar, and getting to know them all in such an atmosphere is just gold."

Part of the job description for new head bartenders is to create a new cocktail menu (though you still can enjoy a White Lady or a Corpse Reviver #2), and the current one created by Schulte and bar manager Declan McGurk is inspired by American music, of all things, from across the years. On creating new drinks, Schulte says, "Making a good drink can start really anywhere! I love being creative as a bartender, this is my only way of letting my creativity and ideas out."

If ever a bar was worth putting on your bucket list, this is it.

- THE JEROME -

This was the first cocktail created by Maxim Schulte when he started as head bartender, among the most coveted positions in the global drinks industry. He credits London legend and American Bar manager Declan McGurk with providing the inspiration for the Jerome, which was conceived in memory of Jerome DuPont, from the famous Calvados-producing DuPont family.

GLASSWARE: Coupe

GARNISH: Strip of lemon peel

- 1½ oz. Calvados VSOP
- 1 teaspoon Suze
- ½ oz. Pierre Ferrand Cognac
- ⅞ oz. verjus
- 2 dashes orange bitters
- 2 teaspoons Rich Simple Syrup (see page 24)
- 2 dashes Peychaud's Bitters
- 1¾ oz. Roederer Estate Brut Champagne, to top

1. Add all of the ingredients, except for the Champagne, to a mixing glass containing a large ice cube, stir until chilled, and strain into the coupe.

2. Top with the Champagne and garnish with the strip of lemon peel.

THE CONNAUGHT BAR AT THE CONNAUGHT HOTEL

CARLOS PLACE
LONDON W1K 2AL

A crown jewel of London's drinks scene, the Connaught is one of the best bars in the world, largely thanks to the efforts of director of mixology Ago Perrone, who redesigned and relaunched the bar 11 years ago (see page 282).

Thanks to a refurbishment led by the renowned designer David Collins, the Connaught's dim lighting soothingly whispers class, a feeling of refinement that also oozes from the silver-leaf walls, dark-leather armchairs, and stunning silver gateways beside the bar.

While Perrone leads the operation, head mixologist Giorgio Bargiani ensures that the bar runs smoothly and to the highest standard. The Connaught consistently creates a number of the world's best cocktails by following its own style and vision, often ignoring the trends emerging in the many bars around it.

Doing this enables Bargiani and his team to foster unique experiences, focusing on the centrality of service: "We want to be recognizable with each and every drink that we do. Every creation is done in our style. It can draw on other influences, but it must be our own. Just as important is that the drinks must connect to the stories they tell our guests and create an experience that they will never forget."

The Connaught's famous Martini is the clearest example of the bar's unique approach to unforgettable experiences. The serving bartender arrives at your table wheeling a sumptuous trolley, applying a classy touch of theater that almost resembles a religious ritual, and then mixes a truly spectacular Martini—quite probably the best you'll have in your life.

– CONNAUGHT MARTINI –

The Connaught Martini, created by Ago Perrone, is legendary worldwide. When ordered at the hotel, it is mixed tableside, adding a superb interactive element to the experience. First, vodka or gin is chosen. Each guest is then asked to smell the aromas of each bitter and choose according to their preference. The signature pour is then held high above the head of the mixologist for the ultimate theatrical touch.

GLASSWARE: Cocktail glass

GARNISH: Lemon twist or an olive

- ½ oz. dry vermouth (the bar uses a blend)
- 2½ oz. gin or vodka (the bar prefers to use Connaught Bar Gin, made, bottled, and sold at the hotel, and Tanqueray No. 10 gin)
- 5 drops bitters (the bar offers cardamom, lavender, liquorice, grapefruit, vanilla, ginger, or coriander seed bitters, but use whatever bitters you have on hand and like best)

1. Chill the cocktail glass.

2. Add the vermouth and chosen spirit to a mixing glass filled with ice and stir until chilled.

3. Coat the chilled glass with the bitters and then strain the cocktail into the glass, with as much distance as possible between the mixing glass and the cocktail glass.

4. Garnish with a lemon twist or an olive.

BAR BANTER
AGO PERRONE
DIRECTOR OF MIXOLOGY
THE CONNAUGHT BAR

Agostino Perrone, better known as Ago, has been the main force behind one of the world's best bars. The Connaught has been perched at the forefront of the global drinks scene for more than a decade, and shows no signs of slipping.

WHAT ORIGINALLY BROUGHT YOU TO THE CONNAUGHT?

The opportunity to open the Connaught Bar came up in 2008 as part of a big refurbishment. The hotel was known for being classy, classic, and very British. They wanted to add an injection of innovation into the hotel bar scene so they looked for the right candidates around London, someone who could bring a balance between a style of service, tradition, elegance, creativity, and innovation.

I was brought in as head mixologist to bring a creative side to what was already a classic environment at the Connaught, with attention to the details and focus on the guest experience. So, really, the aim from the beginning was balancing the guest experience with the creativity. It was not easy in the beginning as there were few bars that were doing freshly squeezed lemon juice, only a few bars applying molecular techniques into their cocktails, and few bars providing personalized service.

HOW DO YOU STAY AT THE FOREFRONT OF DRINKS INNOVATION, ESPECIALLY AS LONDON HAS BECOME MORE SATURATED WITH HIGH-QUALITY COCKTAIL BARS?

I think that a lot of people get stressed because they want to be seen as the most innovative place. Our emphasis is on our guests, that they feel like there is always something special going on, no matter how many times they visit. So, we're at the forefront of our own innovation. We do respect what other people do, but we will never copy what anyone else does.

Lately, we found our inspiration just simply from what is happening in this room. The menu that we launched to celebrate our 11th anniversary is inspired by the structure of the bar itself. Inspiration can come from simple things that surround you, that you don't pay attention to until somebody makes you notice. There are so many little details that aren't highlighted here at the Connaught Bar, but it makes the difference when the story is told and it comes alive for our guests.

HOW DO YOU MAKE A GREAT MARTINI?

With a smile!

The attitude of its creator will make its way into the quality of the drinks. You and I can make exactly the same cocktail, with the same ingredients, with the same ice, cut in the same way, pouring the ingredients in the same order, stir it the same amount of times. But when you pour it into the glass, the drinks will be different. The attitude and the passion that you put into what you do is the key.

And it's not about approaching it as: "I'm making the best Martini." No. It's about "I'm making *your* best Martini," with the attention on the guest. Making a Martini is very simple and there are lots of variants. However, in the same way a chef works with fire, we work with ice. The ice is the tool of the trade here, as well as an ingredient. With ice, you provide the dilution, you give the perfect balance between temperature and mouthfeel.

At the Connaught, our two main ingredients are technicality and a bit of theatrical entertainment. That's the secret of our Martini. You'll only need to try it to see the secret for yourself.

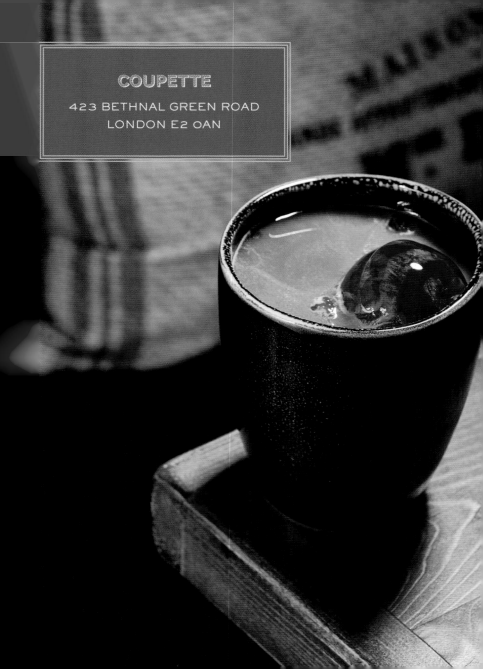

COUPETTE

423 BETHNAL GREEN ROAD
LONDON E2 0AN

– DIABLO OTOÑO –

This is a light but surprisingly complex drink, thanks to creator Andrei Marcu. The green notes of the tequila work very well with the light and refreshing notes coming from the fig cordial, which contains both fig leaves and fresh figs. Topping it all up with tonic provides a slightly bitter finish.

GLASSWARE: Highball glass
GARNISH: None

- 1 oz. Tapatio Blanco
- 1 oz. Fig Cordial
- 1 teaspoon fig liqueur
- Tonic water, to top

1. Add all of the ingredients, except for the tonic water, to a highball glass containing three ice spheres and stir until chilled.

2. Top with the tonic water.

FIG LEAF SYRUP: Place 30 fig leaves in a container. Make Simple Syrup (see page 24), using 25 oz. of water and 25 oz. of sugar. When the syrup is ready to be removed from heat, pour it over the fig leaves and steep for 30 minutes before straining and bottling.

FIG CORDIAL: Preheat oven to 350°F. Quarter 15 figs, place them on a parchment-lined baking sheet, cover the figs with 3½ oz. honey, and then sprinkle 1¾ oz. walnuts around the pan. Bake for 10 minutes. Pour all of the Fig Leaf Syrup into a saucepan and heat it over medium heat. When the figs are done, add them to the syrup and simmer for 10 minutes. Strain into a container and stir in 1 tablespoon of citric acid and, if desired, 7 oz. of Rosé. Let cool completely before using or storing.

FAM BAR

The term "fam" is often heard in London slang, signifying family or someone close. It also was the name of a fruit-and-vegetable shop beloved by co-founders Megs Miller and Dre Masso. They dreamed up FAM Bar to provide a cozy and relaxed space that can be enjoyed by all comers, nestled next to the shopping wonderland of Oxford Street. "We are in an area that is surrounded by mostly restaurants and Selfridges [department store]," says Miller. "So, we have simply focused on being the neighborhood bar to go to before and after dinner, or after shopping."

The bar is their tribute to the legacy and philosophy of legendary London bartender Dick Bradsell (see page 14), creating drinks that are seasonal and easily reproducible, and using sustainable, organic ingredients and materials whenever possible. Drawing on her university education in interior design, Miller worked up the bar using furniture discovered in antique stores, with plenty of vinyl records decorating the walls.

FAM Bar is known for its Margaritas, but also uses local ingredients and spirits for many of its cocktails. That ethos of sustainability informs its menu of small plates and tapas as well. However, the secret to FAM Bar's success is its intimate atmosphere, of which Miller is justifiably proud: "We want every single person who walks through our doors to feel welcome. We focus on warm, friendly service, feel-good vinyl that the guests can flip through and choose what they want to listen to, and tasty drinks."

– FAM MARGARITA –

This drink is inspired by the time FAM co-founder Megs Miller spent a Mexican Independence Day alongside many tequileros at a friend's family restaurant. Multiple brands were combined into a pitcher and then shared with everyone, a wonderful representation of what tequila and Mexican hospitality are all about.

GLASSWARE: Rocks glass

GARNISH: Lemon thyme sprig

- 1¾ oz. tequila blend (Olmeca Altos Plata, Tequila Ocho Plata, Fortaleza Reposado)
- ¾ oz. fresh lemon juice
- ⅞ oz. Devon Flower Honey Water (1 part wildflower honey to 1 part water, stirred together)

1. Add all of the ingredients to a cocktail shaker filled with ice, shake vigorously until chilled, and double-strain over ice into a rocks glass.

2. Garnish with the sprig of lemon thyme.

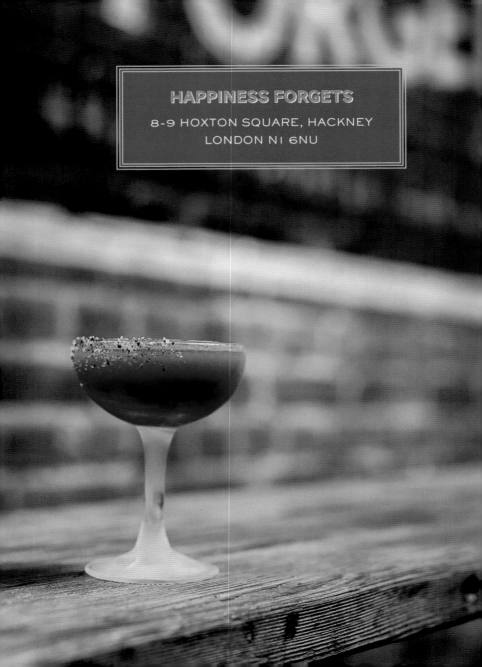

HAPPINESS FORGETS

8-9 HOXTON SQUARE, HACKNEY
LONDON N1 6NU

- I WILL SURVIVE -

This classed-up Bloody Mary owes its success to bar manager Giancarlo Jesus's decision to include Chartreuse, which helps punch up the natural vegetal qualities of this classic pick-me-up. As you can guess from the name, this is the drink of choice when you feel like life, or your hangover, is grinding you down.

GLASSWARE: Coupette

GARNISH: None

- 1 teaspoon chipotle powder
- 1 teaspoon salt, plus more to taste
- 1 oz. Green Chartreuse
- 1 oz. fresh lime juice
- 2½ oz. tomato juice
- 3 dashes Worcestershire sauce
- 3 dashes Tabasco Chipotle Pepper Sauce
- Black pepper, to taste
- 2 dashes celery bitters

1. Chill the coupette.

2. Place the chipotle powder and the salt in a saucer and stir to combine. Wet the rim of the coupette and dip it into the mixture.

3. Add the remaining ingredients to the glass and stir to combine.

BAR BANTER
GIANCARLO JESUS, BAR MANAGER
HAPPINESS FORGETS

Named for a Dionne Warwick lyric, Happiness Forgets used to be a spare room for a Thai restaurant. Now, it's one of London's top hole-in-the-wall bars, known and respected by the city's drinks industry. It's up to bar manager Giancarlo Jesus to ensure that the venue keeps up the high standards that have made Happiness Forgets an institution for the past eight years.

YOU CAME IN AFTER THE BAR HAD ALREADY ESTABLISHED ITSELF AS A TOP VENUE. WAS THAT HARD?

When I came in, the idea was to stick with the formula, run with it, and make sure that nothing kind of broke down. When you've got something good going, why try and mend it?

The owner himself [bar entrepreneur Alastair Burgess] has a really good idea of what he perceives as service and how to run a bar. I've been quite fortunate that I've worked with a lot of people like that. I like to think in my mind I have that same mindset. It means that we see eye to eye about where we think the bar should go, which is great.

WHILE THE MENU CHANGES, THERE ARE THREE DRINKS THAT HAVE BEEN ON THE MENU FOR MANY YEARS. WHAT ARE THEY?

We have a menu of 12 drinks and three signature serves. They are the Tokyo Collins, The Perfect Storm, and the Jerezana.

The Tokyo Collins is a fresh, tall gin cocktail, which uses fresh grapefruit, fresh lemon, and a little bit of soda.

The Perfect Storm, as implied in the name, is a riff on a Dark and Stormy. It uses Skipper's Rum, a little plum eau de vie, fresh ginger juice, a touch of lemon, and a bit of honey. That plum eau de vie just adds a lot of orchard fruit and it's quite delicious.

Then there's the Jerezana. That is a blend of Manzanilla Amontillado Sherry with some dry and sweet vermouth, a touch of vanilla and orange bitters. It's very simple, a cross between two vermouth classics, the Adonis and the Bamboo. I'm a big fan of sherry, so I'm a sucker for this one. When I first started, I thought that it was one of the best drinks I've ever had.

YOU GUYS HAVE DONE TAKEOVERS ALL OVER THE WORLD. WHERE HAVE YOU TRAVELED TO?

Thanks to the reputation of the owner and the reputation of the bar, we've been approached by a lot of people. Earlier this year, I had the opportunity to go to Dubai, which is definitely somewhere that I never thought I'd be able to see and experience. Russia as well, and it's the same idea: we headed over to do a presentation about the bar, our ethos and style of service. And then we just go and make drinks for people, just like any other shift.

Last year, our head bartender and our owner were in Shanghai for a drinks magazine award ceremony. They did a takeover and a presentation there, too. It's just amazing to see that a small little basement bar in East London can still make a bit of noise around the world.

KOSMOPOL

138 FULHAM ROAD
SOUTH KENSINGTON
LONDON SW10 9PY

– DALKULLA –

*D*alkulla is the Swedish term for women from the region of Dalarna. Inspired by Scandinavian spices and herbs, Fredrik Olsson's Dalkulla is aromatic yet silky smooth. The aromas should remind you of walking in a pine forest.

GLASSWARE: Wine glass

GARNISH: Rosemary sprig dusted with confectioners' sugar

- 1¼ oz. aquavit
- 2 teaspoons Metté Liqueur Bourgeons de Sapin
- 1¼ oz. fresh lemon juice
- 2 teaspoons Simple Syrup (see page 24)
- 1 egg white

1. Add all of the ingredients to a cocktail shaker containing no ice. Dry shake for 15 seconds, add ice, and shake vigorously until chilled.

2. Strain into the wine glass and garnish with the rosemary sprig dusted with confectioners' sugar.

BAR BANTER
FREDRIK OLSSON
FOUNDER AND OWNER, KOSMOPOL

An award-winning bartender, Fredrik Olsson is best known for his Chelsea institution, Kosmopol, though it is just one of his many projects. He's also a brand ambassador for Ballantine's whisky, he previously directed a bartending school, and his array of skills has allowed him to provide five-star service to plenty of A-list celebrities over the years.

WHERE DID THE BAR NAME COME FROM?

The name was extremely hard to come up with at the time. There were four of us originally—I'm on my own now. I bought the guys out throughout the years—and it took ages to figure out what we'd use.

So, at the time, in the early 2000s, the Cosmopolitan was popular, but the word also means that you're worldly and well-travelled. So the name was a shortening of that word to show that we wanted to welcome people from all over the world. But remember, it's Kosmopol with a "K." A lot of people get that wrong.

KOSMOPOL WASN'T ALWAYS A NEIGHBORHOOD BAR. HOW DID THAT DEVELOP?

We've found our local regulars come back over and over again, and you do that through consistency and quality. The people are the most important thing and creating that atmosphere is so important for us.

I'm Swedish, so there is a bit of a Swedish angle to what we do with our events, ingredients, and cocktails. It's a light influence. We don't shove it in your face. It's about the clients here, though, so if you want a Gin & Tonic, of course we'll do that for you.

We opened in 2002, and it was a different bar scene than now. The global scene was more centered in London and we set out to be recognized as one of the best bars in the city, which we were. We were nominated for loads of awards—though we never won any—but we were always in the running back then.

We did, however, get the *Time Out* Love London award in 2016, which recognized standout neighborhood bars. It says a bit about how we've changed over time. When we started, we aimed to compete with the top bars, but as we settled in we realized the most important thing is the locals. And they don't want you to change all the time. They don't want you to do the coolest thing. They want what they like to drink, and they like the classics with a little bit of a fun twist behind them.

YOU'RE LOCATED IN CHELSEA. HOW HAS THAT SHAPED THE KOSMOPOL OVER THE YEARS?

Chelsea used to be very clean-cut. You wouldn't see tattoos or piercings, and it was even frowned upon for bartenders to have these in this posh area. It's very different now. Chelsea has also gotten more relaxed and friendlier; I've found that people have gotten more flexible about trying different things.

Also, you know the TV show *Made in Chelsea*? It sounds silly, but that's actually brought a lot of people over here. We also do get some celebrities who come here, a few soccer players, Prince William and Kate Middleton have been here, too. Chelsea is a place that these kinds of people can go out without being harassed.

LYANESS

20 UPPER GROUND
SOUTH BANK
LONDON SE1 9P

This full-bodied cocktail was improvised on the spot for me when I visited Lyaness and head bartender Will Meredith heard that I was fond of Scotch whisky. The result is simple and delicious. Here's the profile in his words: "You often get pear and chocolate in certain blended Scotches so that's accentuated here with the addition of the pear liqueur and cacao. That's then balanced out by the Amontillado Sherry and the bitters."

GLASSWARE: Coupe

GARNISH: Lemon twist

- 1¾ oz. blended Scotch whisky (Monkey Shoulder is a great choice)
- 2 teaspoons Amontillado Sherry
- 1½ teaspoons pear liqueur
- 1 teaspoon white cacao liqueur
- 1 teaspoon Cointreau
- ½ teaspoon Rich Simple Syrup (see page 24)
- 2 dashes Angostura Bitters

1. Add all of the ingredients to the coupe, stir to combine, and garnish with the lemon twist.

BAR BANTER
RYAN CHETIYAWARDANA
OWNER AND FOUNDER, LYANESS

One of the best-known names in London bartending, Ryan Chetiyawardana (better-known as "Mr. Lyan") first shook up the industry by creating drinks in batches, without ice or citrus, in order to emphasize quality of service. With each of his projects, he has found a new angle on how drinks are conceived and created while focusing on sustainability. When his bar Dandelyan was declared "Best Bar" at the 2018 Tales of the Cocktail Festival, Chetiyawardana announced its closure and has since replaced it with Lyaness.

WHAT WAS YOUR MIXOLOGY AND ENTREPRENEURSHIP EDUCATION BEFORE OPENING YOUR FIRST BAR?

I originally started in kitchens. Over my career, I've worked in pretty much every position covering pubs, fine dining, small cocktail bars, boutique hotels, nightclubs, and five-star hotels. I've taken little bits from all of them—good and bad—but I was thankful to have some great mentors along the way. I was also able to explore lots of different sides to what I loved: hosting and creating great drinks at (Edinburgh, Scotland, bar) Bramble, running the lab and R & D at 69 Colebrooke Row, to leading the creative development of the Whistling Shop.

HOW DOES LYANESS REFLECT YOUR OVERALL PHILOSOPHY TO COCKTAIL CREATION?

I say we create "accessible innovation," but really, we like to create beautiful and comfortable places that feel exciting for people to gather with their family and friends. But it needs to balance—although we like the weirder side of things, and something that feels different and special, we want to make sure it feels relevant and honest to people.

Within each of the venues, we're always trying to challenge and kick off a discussion. We use everything in our control to address this—the setting, the music, the lighting, the set-up for the team and, of course, the food and drink. We try and create platforms for the team to shine and with Lyaness I believe we've really hit that. It's an incredible space, but we have the best team in the world; they've created something that feels very distinct to the global drinking scene and have made it accessible to everyone—not just cocktail geeks.

YOU'VE PUSHED HARD FOR SUSTAINABILITY INITIATIVES IN THE HOSPITALITY SUPPLY CHAIN. HOW DOES BEING IN LONDON AFFECT WHAT YOU DO IN THIS REGARD?

Sustainability has been a pillar of the company for the last 10 years and London poses some challenges and opportunities for this. In one sense, the platform, the critical mass, and the engagement mean we have a greater opportunity to instigate positive change. The growing number of kindred spirits means we can pool resources, but London still poses problems. We are removed from farmers and costs are incredibly high. So, it also poses challenges that other spaces don't have to navigate.

WHAT MAKES LONDON STAND OUT TO YOU AS A COCKTAIL CITY?

London is the most diverse city in the world, but it's also a global hub for finance, tech, fashion, and the arts, which all leads to creating the most dynamic food-and-drink scene on the planet. Coupled with the fact that people from across the world are able to work here, and are attracted to working here, it means there's an unprecedented dynamic among communities here.

SWIFT

12 OLD COMPTON STREET
SOHO, LONDON W1D 4TQ

Edinburgh native Bobby Hiddleston and Swede Mia Johnansson may be London's most celebrated bartending couple. Both benefit from significant experience working in London's hippest institutions (also, Hiddleston was the first head bartender at New York's Dead Rabbit), and now they dedicate that expertise to their (relatively) new bar Swift, collaborating with similarly decorated husband-and-wife team Edmund Weil and Rosie Stimpson of both Nightjar and Oriole.

Swift is dedicated to minimalist drinks. "Keep things simple as much as you can," says Hiddleston. "It's better to have two flavors that work perfectly together than eight that are all kind of okay."

Swift is divided into two experiences: upstairs, a casual bar emphasizes aperitif cocktails. Downstairs features an impressive whisky bar, replete with whisky cocktails as well as a few other creative drinks incorporating spirits from around the world, and live jazz and blues on weekends.

Focusing on innovation and simplicity, Swift stands out not just in London's competitive drinks scene. It has grown into a mainstay for Soho's regulars and residents—and that's important to Hiddleston: "Soho has so many different demographics of people. For being in the center of London, it has a very local vibe and the residents are fiercely protective of its identity. We wanted to fit in and not dilute that, so it was very important from the beginning that we have a strong relationship with our community."

- PICCOLINA -

The balance between the dry and sweet white Port and the Rancio-esque Amontillado really helps this drink stand out. It's also an excellent example of bar co-owner Bobby Hiddleston's philosophy of keeping things simple in order to create excellent cocktails.

GLASSWARE: Cocktail glass

GARNISH: Green olive

- 2 oz. dry white Port
- 1 oz. Amontillado Sherry
- ½ oz. fig liqueur
- 3 dashes Angostura Bitters

1. Add all of the ingredients to a mixing glass filled with ice, stir until chilled, and strain into the cocktail glass.

2. Garnish with the green olive.

TAYĒR + ELEMENTARY

- PALO SANTO GIMLET -

This refreshing, easy-to-drink, yet complex cocktail was inspired by a trip Tayēr + Elementary co-founder Alex Kratena made to the Amazon rainforest. It is in the style of a Gimlet, but the palo santo adds an additional level of complexity. Palo santo is a sacred South American tree; it literally means "holy wood."

GLASSWARE: Yakisugi glass or a rocks glass
GARNISH: Lemon twist

- 1¾ oz. Tayēr X Hepple Gin (as this gin is made for the bar, use a craft gin of your choosing)
- ½ oz. Fino Sherry
- ½ oz. Lillet Blanc
- ½ oz. Palo Santo Cordial

1. Add all of the ingredients to a mixing glass filled with ice, stir until chilled, and strain over a single block of ice into the chosen glass.

2. Garnish with the lemon twist.

PALO SANTO CORDIAL (MAKES 1¾ CUPS): In a saucepan over low heat, combine 2 teaspoons palo santo extract, 5 cups sugar, 5 teaspoons citric acid, and 5 cups water and stir gently until sugar dissolves; don't let the mixture come to a simmer. Once sugar has dissolved, remove pan from heat and let cool completely before using or storing.

THREE SHEETS

510B KINGSLAND ROAD
DALSTON, LONDON E8 4AB

At first glance, Three Sheets appears to be an unassuming, but chic, hole-in-the-wall in East London's hip Dalston neighborhood, not a bar repeatedly celebrated as one of the best in the world by Tales of the Cocktail and the World's 50 Best Bars (#16 in 2019). Mancunian brothers Max and Noel Venning opened the place in 2016 on a small budget and have been on the rise ever since. Noel says all it took to move to London to join his brother was "one phone call from Max to me. He said he had found a site and asked if I was up for it, to which I obviously said 'Yes.'"

Unassuming is also an apt description of their cocktail philosophy. "Our approach is very simple," says Noel. "We concentrate on a specific flavor then build a drink from there." This minimalist approach has earned the brothers endless praise, with reason. The Almond Flower Sour, for example, is a fluffy, creamy pillow filled with subtle, flowery nuance made with four ingredients: almond flour, egg white, gin, and lemon juice. The Shiso Miso, on the other hand, takes Japanese flavors and distills them into cocktail form.

Despite the international recognition, Noel regards his little joint as a friendly, easygoing neighborhood bar: "Being where we are has definitely given us a neighborhood feel. We have an amazing base of regulars who live in the area around the bar and come in at least once a week—sometimes three or four times a week—some of whom have become very good friends."

– SHISO MISO –

Fat-washing is a great way of adding another dimension to spirits, giving them an irresistible depth. This particular drink, which features fat-washed whisky, hasn't left the Three Sheets menu since co-owner Noel Venning opened the place in 2016. It's best prepared in a larger quantity and kept in a bottle in the fridge, but this recipe is for a single cocktail.

GLASSWARE: Rocks glass or ceramic mug
GARNISH: Shiso leaf

- 1¾ oz. Fat-Washed Nikka Days Whisky
- 1¾ teaspoons Rich Simple Syrup (see page 24)

- 6 dashes Angostura Bitters

1. Add all of ingredients to a mixing glass filled with ice, stir until chilled, and strain over ice cubes into the chosen glass.

2. Garnish with the shiso leaf.

FAT-WASHED NIKKA DAYS WHISKY: Pour 1¾ cups Nikka Days (or another good, unpeated malt whisky) into a large Tupperware container or half-gallon jug. In a saucepan over medium heat, melt 5 tablespoons unsalted butter and then stir in ¼ oz. white miso paste and ¼ oz. fresh shiso leaves. When the butter starts to brown, remove pan from heat and pour the mixture into the whisky. Stir until everything is thoroughly combined then tightly seal with plastic wrap (and put plastic wrap on before placing the top on the Tupperware container if that's what you're using). Freeze overnight, or until all the butter has risen to the top and solidified into a solid layer. Scrape away the butter solids and strain the whisky before using or storing.

DISTILLERIES

BEEFEATER NEGRONI • GREEN PARK •

RE-CHARRED OLD FASHIONED •

THE RENEGADE SOUTHSIDE •

FRANKIE MANGOES TO HOLLYWOOD •

HIGHGATE CEMETERY #1 •

HEMINGWAY'S CABBY DAIQUIRI

n 2010, there were a mere 23 distilleries in all of England. Nine years later, that number rocketed to 166 confirmed facilities, with London home to at least 25, a sign the craft spirits boom has taken a solid hold in the UK.

Driven mainly by the gin explosion, a few of these distilleries have diversified their portfolio. Many also produce vodka, flavored spirits, and rum, and some are even creating superb whiskies.

No two distilleries are alike. Most, with the exception of Beefeater, are smaller, independent operations, each taking its own approach to the distillation process. Here is a showcase of what some of those distilleries are doing and the irresistible cocktails that can be made with their products.

BEEFEATER

20 MONTFORD PLACE, OVAL, LONDON SE11 5DE

The largest and oldest gin distillery in London, Beefeater has been in production since 1863. The legendary name refers to the red-clad Yeomen Warders who serve as the ceremonial guards at the Tower of London.

The distillery is overseen by master distiller Desmond Payne, gin's elder statesman, who last year was awarded an MBE and celebrated 50 years in the gin industry. He has been pleasantly surprised by the current boom: "Since I've been here, especially in the last 10 years, there's been a whole regeneration of interest in gin. The excitement around it is terrific."

Reacting to the changing gin market, Beefeater launched various new gins with different profiles over the years, including Beefeater 24 and the Burrough's Reserve. Payne prefers to adopt a subtler approach when conceiving a new gin: "To create something new is, on the surface, quite easy, as you just have to change one ingredient. But I've learned that creating a new gin, or a new variety of an existing gin, requires a gentle touch. The most important lesson is not to overdo it."

Though Beefeater has been in its current facility since 1958, the actual production recipe has remained primarily unchanged since the 19th century. Not only is it one of the first London Dry gins, but Beefeater also claims to be the "World's Most Awarded Gin." Here's to many more centuries of Beefeater as a leading light of gin production.

– BEEFEATER NEGRONI –

A classic Negroni recipe using Beefeater Gin, this is a favorite of Beefeater master distiller Desmond Payne. The Negroni is hugely popular in all the major cities, and London is no different, as evidenced by the few interesting twists that appear in this book. That said, there is a reason this is a true classic—in this case, because it is made with a classic gin.

GLASSWARE: Rocks glass

GARNISH: Orange twist

- 1 part Beefeater London Dry Gin
- 1 part Campari
- 1 part sweet vermouth

1. Add all of the ingredients to a mixing glass filled with ice and stir until chilled.

2. Strain into a rocks glass containing a block of ice.

3. Garnish with an orange twist.

BERMONDSEY DISTILLERY (JENSEN'S GIN)

55 STANWORTH STREET
BERMONDSEY, LONDON SE1 3NY

Christian Jensen's professional journey with gin began in a bar in Tokyo, where he was able to taste and compare two gins of the same brand that were released a few decades apart. The old bottle clearly was the better product, and that was a revelation for Jensen.

Years later and now living in London, he convinced gin expert and distiller Charles Maxwell to make some gin following the flavor profile of the better spirit he had tasted back then: "He said that making gin would be a silly thing to do; that it should be whisky or vodka as that's what everyone was drinking at the time. But he saw I was passionate and we ended up making a recipe together. That was my first London Dry."

However, due to the tax code, he was not actually allowed to buy the gin from Maxwell. That meant Jensen had to form a company in order to buy directly from a distillery. Hence, the birth of Bermondsey Gin Ltd.: "I ended up getting 1,200 bottles that I realized I probably should try to sell rather than keep to myself. So I would wander around to pubs and shops. Eventually, I found a shop that took the stock and managed to shift it."

Since that first run, Jensen not only built his own distillery in Bermondsey, but also has become one of the city's top authorities on gin and its history. He prioritizes historical accuracy to be able to produce two top-quality gins, a London Dry and an Old Tom, drawing on traditional recipes: "I managed to track down recipes from the 19th century and I wanted to make a historically accurate gin as I had known it in the past."

- GREEN PARK -

Erik Lorincz is the former head bartender at the American Bar at The Savoy, and currently runs the acclaimed bar Kwānt. This is one of his most iconic creations, made to work with Jensen's Old Tom Gin, the vivid, pea-green Green Park. A twist on a White Lady (see page 41), this silky-smooth gin cocktail also adds herbal and citric elements not typically found in the original.

GLASSWARE: Coupe

GARNISH: None

- 2 basil leaves
- 1½ oz. Jensen's Old Tom Gin
- 1 oz. fresh lemon juice
- ½ oz. Simple Syrup (see page 24)
- 3 drops Bittermens Orchard Street Celery Shrub
- 2 teaspoons egg white

1. Slap the basil leaves to awaken the aromatics. Add them to a cocktail shaker along with ice and the remaining ingredients. Shake vigorously until chilled.

2. Strain into the coupe.

BIMBER

It's no exaggeration to say that the single-malt whisky coming out of Bimber (Polish for "moonshine") has the whisky world very excited. Founder Dariusz Plazewski certainly knows what he's doing: "I'm a third-generation distiller from Poland. I learned about it from my grandfather and father, who essentially made moonshine. In Poland, everything was done by instinct, through touch and smell, with barely any equipment to make something that you can drink straightaway. This is how I learned the craft."

Plazewski has a singular, ambitious vision to produce a single malt: "I wanted to craft a whisky that is as local as possible and as close to the old-fashioned way of production as possible. We get all our barley crop from a single farm, around an hour from London, and our malting is done nearby at Warminster Maltings as well."

Bimber has recently doubled its production capacity, with plans to expand further and to build new facilities around its West London location.

Plazewski is so devoted to the idea of producing single-malt whisky that Bimber has even cut production of the critically acclaimed gins, vodkas, and rums the distillery specialized in while waiting for its whisky to mature. There is one exception that survived the cull: "Our big hit has been our Oolong tea gin. We designed the profile of the gin to be able to take an Oolong tea infusion, which lasts seven days and then is left for a month to marry and come together."

With Bimber's whisky already receiving praise at only three years old, it will be exciting to chart its development as older liquid is released.

- RE-CHARRED OLD FASHIONED -

The Old Fashioned is a venerable cocktail, strong but not too strong, sweet but not too sweet. Most of all, it's simple and delicious. Bimber's Re-Charred Single Malt, with its rich, punchy and fruity flavors, enhances the classic, making for a perfectly balanced cocktail with just two ingredients (though the syrup requires a little prep work). This simple serve is the work of brand ambassador Luke Juranek.

GLASSWARE: Rocks glass

GARNISH: Orange twist and a lemon twist

- **2 oz. Bimber Re-Charred Single Malt London Whisky**
- **2 teaspoons Orange & Angostura Syrup**

1. Add the whisky and syrup to a rocks glass containing a large block of ice and stir to combine.

2. Garnish with the orange and lemon twists.

ORANGE & ANGOSTURA SYRUP (MAKES 4 OZ., ADJUST AMOUNTS AS NEEDED): Place 3 oz. water, ¾ oz. Angostura Bitters, 5 oz. caster sugar, and an entire orange peel in a saucepan and cook over low heat, stirring until the sugar has dissolved. Remove from heat and let cool completely before using or storing.

DOGHOUSE DISTILLERY

UNIT L, LONDON STONE BUSINESS ESTATE
BROUGHTON STREET, BATTERSEA, LONDON SW8 3QR

The Doghouse Distillery stands out from most other distillation operations with its production process. "We are London's only full grain-to-bottle distillery. We mill, brew, ferment, and distill; on site," says Australian founder and director Braden Saunders. Though his background in the industry was running the first craft beer pub in Brisbane, Australia—which came after a career in finance—a life-changing trip to Louisville, Kentucky, made Saunders realize he wanted to be distilling.

Doghouse's gin and vodka is made with spirit produced at the distillery itself, with grain brought in from eastern England's Norwich instead of from neutral alcohol spirit bought from an outside producer (as most spirits distilleries do it). Though Doghouse began production in 2017, it draws inspiration from the first American craft distilleries that began production in the '80s—the forerunners of the "craft" category.

Because of their work with both gin and vodka, drawn from a similar base spirit, Saunders prefers to label Doghouse differently than other operations: "We're a grain distillery rather than a gin distillery. The whole aim was to be a West Coast American craft distillery, to specialize in grains rather than a "gin" concept." In addition to its Renegade gin, Doghouse's Baller vodka won "Best Spirit" at the Great British Food Awards. The distillery also produces sweeter sloe and damson gins.

- THE RENEGADE SOUTHSIDE -

This is a standard recipe for a Southside cocktail—in this case using Doghouse Distillery's Renegade Gin. Allegedly, the cocktail was a favorite of bootlegging mobster Al Capone, for whom the Southside was made in order to cope with the punchy gin that he preferred.

GLASSWARE: Coupe

GARNISH: Mint leaf

- 1 handful mint leaves
- 2 oz. Doghouse Renegade Gin
- 1 oz. fresh lime juice
- ¾ oz. Simple Syrup (see page 24)

1. Chill the coupe.

2. Slap the mint leaves to awaken the aromatics. Add them, ice, and all of the remaining ingredients to a cocktail shaker and shake vigorously until chilled.

3. Double-strain into the chilled coupe and garnish with an additional mint leaf.

EAST LONDON LIQUOR COMPANY

BOW WHARF, UNIT GF1
221 GROVE ROAD, LONDON E3 5SN

Located in a former glue factory, the East London Liquor Company has gone from strength to strength. Starting with a team of four, it now employs more than 40 people and sells its products across 20 international markets. "We're making gins, vodkas, and a few whiskies as well," says global brand ambassador Mikey Pendergast (one of the four original team members). "We're one of the first in London for quite a long time. And we also import our own proprietary rum from Guyana. The idea is we want to make spirits that we would drink ourselves."

Despite its rapid growth, the ELLC is always happy to experiment with unusual spirits. Even its gin options are the result of happy squabbling among the team, according to communications manager Ashley Hunka: "We took our two final candidate recipes for a premium gin to bartenders we knew to decide their favorite and it ended up being a 50/50 split. So we released both. One is very dry, it makes for an excellent, dry Martini. The other is herbaceous, punchy, and savory, like an English herb garden. This is the Negroni gin, it holds up well against Campari."

The ELLC's also broken a whisky milestone, releasing the first whisky, a rye, made in London's East End since the closure of the Lea Valley Distillery in 1903. Following a successful round of crowdfunding, the distillery has doubled its whisky production, and Hunka says there are no plans to change its maverick approach: "We don't really have much of an emphasis on heritage or using recipes found in our grandparents' chests. We mean that in the nicest way possible. For us, it's just about 'Hey, what do you guys think of this? Should we give it a go?'"

— FRANKIE MANGOES —
TO HOLLYWOOD

From the distillers to the bartenders, the team at East London Liquor Company has a *slight* obsession with hot sauce. Tired of simply adding it to their staff lunches, global brand ambassador Mikey Pendergast decided it would be a kick to drink it, too. Enter the Frankie Mangoes to Hollywood.

GLASSWARE: Coupe

GARNISH: Dried raspberry dust

- 1¾ oz. Earl Grey-Infused East London Liquor Company London Dry Gin
- ¾ oz. fresh lemon juice
- ½ oz. Monin Mango Syrup
- 1 teaspoon Frank's RedHot
- 1 egg white, ¾ oz. aquafaba, or 2 drops Mrs. Better's Bitters Miraculous Foamer

1. Add all of the ingredients to a cocktail shaker filled with ice and shake vigorously until chilled.

2. Double-strain into the coupe.

3. Top with a few sprinkles of raspberry dust.

EARL GREY-INFUSED EAST LONDON LIQUOR COMPANY LONDON DRY GIN: Place 2 bags (or ⅛ oz. loose-leaf) of Earl Grey tea in a 750 ml bottle of East London Liquor Company London Dry Gin. Steep until the gin is tinted and the bergamot is evident on the nose, about 5 minutes. Remove the tea bags (or strain) before using or storing, taking care not to press the tea to remove more liquid.

SACRED SPIRITS

50 HIGHGATE HIGH STREET
LONDON N6 5HX

Sacred Spirits began in 2009 as a distillery located in the Highgate home of founders and married couple Ian Hart and Hilary Whitney. Only recently did they actually move into a dedicated facility to expand production of their award-winning spirits. "Having distilled in our home for the past 10 years, we are looking forward to opening new premises on Highgate High Street, which we hope will bring more visitors to the area and footfall for other businesses," says Hilary.

Producing many different gins, vodka, and vermouth (as well as dabbling with some whiskey experiments), the distillery stands out for its unique method of handling ingredients. All botanicals are macerated in English wheat spirit for 4 to 6 weeks. Each is then distilled separately, before being blended together again for a specific Sacred product. The Sacred library holds over 100 botanicals that the distillery can work with in order to experiment and create new flavors. Using a vacuum-distillation process (compared to a pot still, for example) also means that botanicals retain freshness and flavor.

The new facility is still in Highgate, and the couple have no plans to leave the area anytime soon, according to Hilary. "We actually see ourselves as a small, global brand, but we'd never want to move the distillery away from Highgate. Ian has lived here on and off all his life and it's nice to be associated with such a historic part of London."

An herbal and citric variation of Harry Craddock's classic Corpse Reviver #2 (see page 42), this drink is named after the cemetery located on the same street as Sacred Spirits' old facility.

GLASSWARE: Cocktail glass

GARNISH: Maraschino cherry

- 2 to 3 drops absinthe
- 1 oz. Sacred Organic Gin
- 1 oz. Sacred English Amber Vermouth
- 1 oz. fresh lemon juice
- 1 oz. orange liqueur

1. Rinse the cocktail glass with the absinthe.

2. Place the remaining ingredients in a cocktail shaker filled with ice, shake vigorously until chilled, and strain into the glass.

3. Garnish with a maraschino cherry.

TAXI SPIRITS COMPANY

HAVEN MEWS, ARCH 412
ST PAUL'S WAY, LONDON E3 4AG

A former London cab driver, Moses Odong made a complete career switch into distilling following some training as a brewer. Even more unusual is that rather than join in the gin boom, he went straight to founding London's first white rum distillery. The microdistillery produces just 1,000 bottles a year but Odong is excited about occupying his unique niche: "With the industry being saturated with craft gin distilleries, we thought it would be a great opportunity to start a new language, the rum language. A rum distillery is unheard of in Central London and bridging that gap in the market is where we thought we could come in."

On paper, this would not necessarily convey confidence about the quality of Odong's Cabby's Rum. But his multiple awards—a gold medal from The Spirits Business' Rum and Caçhaca Masters competition, and silver from the IWSC after receiving an "outstanding" score from the judging panel—ease any anxiety. Odong owes some of his success to his avoidance of incorporating additional ingredients, a problem that plagues the rum industry. "Like traditional rums, we produce our Cabby's rum from cane molasses only," he says. "We do not add any sugar, syrup, or other source of carbohydrates to increase the level of alcohol, which means it creates more flavors, and it's the craft to balance them for fullest enjoyment."

The result is a rich and full-bodied rum, combining black treacle thickness, a rich taste of coconut, and citrus sweetness.

However, Cabby's hasn't entirely missed the gin explosion. Cabby's Gin was the fruit of experimentation with juniper and pimento berries for a spiced rum, and it became their new gin instead.

Ernest Hemingway helped create this immortal twist on a Daiquiri when he called for more rum and less sugar while living in Havana, Cuba. The drink was confirmed when El Floridita's head bartender Antonio Meilán added maraschino cherry liqueur and grapefruit juice. A little sugar and grapefruit bitters have been added here to enhance the contrast between sweet and sour, as well as amplify the award-winning Cabby's White Rum.

GLASSWARE: Coupette

GARNISH: Lime wedge

- 2 oz. Cabby's White Rum
- 1 oz. fresh lime juice
- ¾ oz. fresh grapefruit juice
- ¾ oz. Simple Syrup (see page 24)
- ¾ oz. maraschino cherry liqueur
- 4 dashes grapefruit bitters

1. Chill the coupette.

2. Add all of the ingredients to a cocktail shaker filled with ice and shake vigorously until chilled.

3. Double-strain into the chilled coupette.

4. Garnish with the lime wedge.

METRIC CONVERSIONS

U.S. Measurement	Approximate Metric Liquid Measurement	Approximate Metric Dry Measurement
1 teaspoon	5 ml	5 g
1 tablespoon or ½ ounce	15 ml	14 g
1 ounce or ⅛ cup	30 ml	29 g
¼ cup or 2 ounces	60 ml	57 g
⅓ cup	80 ml	76 g
½ cup or 4 ounces	120 ml	113 g
⅔ cup	160 ml	151 g
¾ cup or 6 ounces	180 ml	170 g
1 cup or 8 ounces or ½ pint	240 ml	227 g
1½ cups or 12 ounces	350 ml	340 g
2 cups or 1 pint or 16 ounces	475 ml	454 g
3 cups or 1½ pints	700 ml	680 g
4 cups or 2 pints or 1 quart	950 ml	908 g

INDEX

ACKNOWLEDGMENTS

I'm immensely grateful to the many individuals who provided the help, counsel and support required for a first-time author. I couldn't have tackled this project without specific contributions from a few selfless people.

First, my thanks to cocktail guru and writer Kurt Maitland, for putting me in touch with Cider Mill Press. One could argue that it's his fault you hold this book in your hands.

My regular partner-in-musical-and-whisky-crime, Paul Archibald, contributed time-consuming details. My father, David Schrieberg, brought his considerable journalism experience to bear with a thorough editing and proofreading of the entire book. I am grateful to my partner Ania, for her excellent and invaluable ideas that infused this project, not to mention her patience with me as I worked my way through the manuscript.

My Cider Mill Press editor, Buzz Poole, earns my gratitude for taking a chance on me, his flexibility with deadlines, and for graceful finishing touches.

Denver & Liely co-founder Denver Cramer and Fat Bear co-owner Gareth Rees were generous with their connections, putting me in touch with bars in London that I was intent on including.

More generally, a huge thank you to the many London bar/pub owners and restaurateurs who contributed all the recipes included here, to everyone who answered all my interview questions—and to the superb bartenders who served me amazing cocktails as I traversed the city.

And lastly, a huge shout-out to all those working hard across the bars of London, dedicated to creating wonderful experiences for their patrons. You are the reason London serves the best drinks in the world.

PHOTOGRAPHY CREDITS

Page 56: courtesy 100 Wardour Street; page 58: courtesy Artesian at the Langham Hotel; page 63: courtesy The Baptist Bar at L'Oscar; page 66: courtesy Cahoots; page 69: courtesy Ceviche; pages 70 and 73: courtesy The Coral Room at the Bloomsbury Hotel; pages 74 and 77: courtesy Fitz's at the Kimpton Fitzroy Hotel; pages 78-79 and 81: courtesy HIDE Below; page 84: courtesy Knight's Bar at Simpson's in the Strand; pages 86: courtesy The Lucky Pig; pages 88 and 91: courtesy Milk & Honey; page 92: courtesy Mr. Fogg's Society of Exploration; page 95: courtesy Mr. Fogg's Gin Parlour; page 96: courtesy Murder Inc.; pages 98 and 101: courtesy Peony Bar in the Opioum Cocktail and Dim Sum Parlour; pages 102 and 105: courtesy Punch Room at the London Edition Hotel; page 106: courtesy Quaglino's; page 108: courtesy Scarfes Bar at The Rosewood Hotel; page 110: courtesy Sketch; page 112: courtesy Purple Bar at Sanderson Hotel; page 114: courtesy Long Bar at Sanderson Hotel; pages 118 and 121: Dennis Lee, courtesy Smith & Whistle at the Sheraton Grand Park Lane Hotel; page 124: courtesy The Wigmore at the Langham Hotel; pages 126 and 128: courtesy Ziggy's at Hotel Cafe Royal; pages 134 and 137: courtesy The 108 Brasserie; page 138: courtesy Blake's Below at Blake's Hotel; page 140: courtesy Goat Chelsea; page 142: courtesy La Maison Remy; page 144: courtesy Opso; page 147: courtesy Pomona's; page 148: courtesy Trailer Happiness; pages 150 and 153: Tom Leishman, courtesy The Courtyard; pages 158 and 160: Addie Chinn, courtesy Black Rock; page 162: Nina Pennick, courtesy Bobby Fitzpatrick; page 164:

courtesy BYOC Camden; pages 166 and 169: courtesy Croque Monsieur at Lost Boys Pizza; pages 170 and 172: Dan Weill, courtesy Drink, Shop & Do; page 175: courtesy The Gibson; page 176: courtesy Keystone Crescent; pages 178 and 181: Lateef Okunnu, courtesy Little Mercies; pages 182 and 185: courtesy Racketeer; pages 186 and 189: courtesy Laki Lane; page 190: courtesy Victory Mansion; page 198: courtesy Batch; pages 201 and 203 courtesy Funkidory; pages 206 and 209: courtesy Gin & Beer; page 212: courtesy Gong Bar at the Shangri-La Hotel; page 214: courtesy Lost and Found; page 216: courtesy Seven at Brixton; page 219: courtesy Tanner & Co.; page 222: courtesy Three Eight Four; pages 228 and 231: courtesy Behind This Wall; pages 232 and 235: courtesy Bokan; pages 236 and 239: Marc Sethi, courtesy Bull in a China Shop; pages 240 and 242: Rory Paterson, courtesy Discount Suit Company; pages 244 and 246: courtesy The Fat Bear; pages 248 and 250: courtesy Hacha; page 252: courtesy Looking Glass Cocktail Club; page 255: courtesy Kym's; page 258: courtesy Map Maison; page 260: courtesy Mrs. Fogg's Dockside Drinkery & Distillery; page 262: courtesy Pearson Room; page 264: courtesy Sager + Wilde; page 266: courtesy Shep's; page 268: Rory Paterson, courtesy The Sun Tavern; pages 274 and 277: courtesy American Bar at Savoy Hotel; pages 278 and 281: courtesy The Connaught Bar at the Connaught Hotel; page 284: courtesy Coupette; pages 286 and 289: courtesy Fam Bar; pages 290 and 292: Samir Sharma, courtesy Happiness Forgets; pages 294 and 296: courtesy Kosmopol; pages 298 and 300: courtesy Lyaness; pages 302 and 304: Addie Chinn, courtesy Swift; page 306: courtesy Tayer + Elementary; page 308: courtesy Three Sheets; pages 312-313, 318-319, and 321: courtesy Bermondsey Distillery; page 316: courtesy Beefeater; pages 322 and 325: courtesy Bimber; pages 326-327 and 328: courtesy Doghouse Distillery; pages 330 and 333: courtesy East London Liquor Company; page 337: courtesy Taxi Spirits Company.

All other images used under official license from Shutterstock.com.

ABOUT THE AUTHOR

Felipe Schrieberg is a dual American-Luxembourgish drinks and spirits writer based in London. He is a Senior Contributor to Forbes.com, for which he writes about whisky and the drinks industry, among many other global industry publications that publish his work. He is also a judge for the World Whisky Awards.

A professional musician as a vocalist and lap steel guitarist, he is one half of The Rhythm and Booze Project, which combines live music and whisky tasting in many creative and unexpected ways. Past projects include making a bass drum out of an entire (empty) barrel of Lagavulin whisky, running a tasting series that uses music to change the taste of whisky itself, and devising a theater show combining live blues with a whisky masterclass that debuted to critical acclaim at the 2019 Edinburgh Fringe Festival.

This is his first book.

—ABOUT CIDER MILL PRESS BOOK PUBLISHERS—

Good ideas ripen with time. From seed to harvest, Cider Mill Press brings fine reading, information, and entertainment together between the covers of its creatively crafted books. Our Cider Mill bears fruit twice a year, publishing a new crop of titles each spring and fall.

CIDER MILL PRESS

BOOK PUBLISHERS

KENNEBUNKPORT, MAINE

"Where Good Books Are Ready for Press"

Visit us on the web at
cidermillpress.com

or write to us at
PO Box 454
12 Spring St.
Kennebunkport, Maine 04046